Hidden Manifestation

The Forbidden System to Reprogram Your Mind, Amplify Attraction, and Create Limitless Wealth

Codex Occulto

© **Copyright 2025 by Codex Occulto - All rights reserved.**

This publication provides accurate and reliable information on the subject matter discussed. It is sold with the understanding that the publisher is not offering legal, accounting, or professional services. For such advice, consult a qualified expert.

No part of this document may be copied, reproduced, stored, or shared—electronically or in print—without written permission from the publisher. All rights reserved.

The content is presented as-is, with no guarantees. The publisher assumes no responsibility for any loss, damage, or consequences resulting from the use or misuse of the information provided.

Trademarks mentioned are the property of their respective owners and are used for identification purposes only. This publication is not affiliated with them.

All copyrights remain with their respective authors unless held by the publisher.
ISBN: 979-8-89965-376-6
Imprint: Staten House

Table of Contents

You're Manifesting All the Time—But Not Always What You Want.................................. 8
Chapter 1: Why the Surface Techniques Aren't Enough.. 12
    The Hidden Conflict Between Conscious Desire and Subconscious Programming 12
    Why Willpower Isn't Enough.. 13
    The Power of Inner Safety and Nervous System Regulation.......................... 14
    Time to Go Deeper... 14
Chapter 2: The Shadow Side of Intention.. 16
    Intentions That Come from Wounds.. 16
    Energetic Sabotage: When Wanting = Pushing Away.................................. 17
    When Your Conscious Intention and Subconscious Identity Clash................. 18
    Intention Must Be Backed by Integration.. 19
Chapter 3: The Nervous System's Role in Manifestation.. 21
    The Body as a Permission System... 21
    Fight, Flight, Freeze… or Receive?... 22
    Regulation Before Expansion.. 23
    Manifestation Is a Somatic Process.. 24
Chapter 4: Energetic Clutter: The Hidden Static in Your Field.................................... 26
    Thought Loops and Mental Overcrowding.. 26
    Relationships That Distort Your Frequency... 27
    Protect the Signal... 29
Chapter 5: Subconscious Patterning and Money, Love, Success................................ 33
    The Love Loop: Repeating Emotional Imprints.. 35
    The Success Pattern: Identity, Worth, and Self-Concept............................. 36
    Awareness Is the First Alchemy... 37
Chapter 6: Emotional Encoding: What You Feel Is What You Call In.......................... 39
    The Hidden Code Beneath Your Desires... 39
    Emotional Repetition Creates Reality... 40
    The Danger of Emotional Bypassing.. 41
    Emotion Is the Bridge Between Inner and Outer.. 42
Chapter 7: Identity Alchemy: Be the One Who Has It... 44
    Self-Concept: The Silent Governor of Reality.. 44

Embodying the Future Self in the Present Moment....................................45
  Letting Go of the Identity That's Attached to the Old Story........................ 46
  Identity Is the Root Frequency... 47
Chapter 8: Vibration ≠ Emotion: The True Frequency Formula.........................49
  Your Vibration Is a Composite Signal.. 49
  How to Measure Alignment (Beyond How You Feel)................................. 50
  Stabilizing Your Frequency Without Bypassing... 52
  Feel It, But Know What You're Really Feeling... 53
Chapter 9: The 3-Phase Manifestation Flow: Feel → Clear → Act......................56
  Feel: Aligning With the Emotional Blueprint.. 56
  Clear: Releasing the Static and Resistance... 57
  Act: Moving From Alignment, Not Anxiety... 58
  Rinse and Repeat, Again and Again... 59
Chapter 10: The Power of Micro-Decisions...61
  Your Life Is Built on Invisible Choices... 61
  Decision Fatigue vs. Decision Precision... 62
  Tiny Acts That Collapse Time... 63
  Aligning the Ordinary with the Extraordinary... 64
Chapter 11: How to Know If It's Working (Even When It Looks Like It's Not)...66
  Shifts in Your Inner Landscape... 66
  Subtle Real-World Feedback... 67
  When It Feels Worse Before It Feels Better.. 68
  Trust the Unseen Growth... 69
Chapter 12: When to Let Go vs. When to Push...71
  The Energetics of Surrender: Letting Go with Intention............................71
  Aligned Effort: When to Push from Power, Not Panic.............................. 72
  Reading the Signals: Timing and Intuitive Momentum............................ 73
  The Dance Between Will and Surrender.. 74
Chapter 13: Trusting the Invisible Timeline..79
  Why Results Come After Identity, Not Before..79
  The Illusion of Stagnation and the Truth of Recalibration........................ 80
  Becoming a Steward of Timing Instead of a Slave to It............................ 82
  The Timeline Is Already Running.. 83
Chapter 14: Magnetic Boundaries = Magnetic Manifestation........................ 84

Boundaries as a Frequency Filter.. 84
Saying No as an Energetic Yes.. 85
Protecting the Field Without Hiding from Life.. 86
Boundaries Are a Manifestation Tool.. 87

Chapter 15: Beyond Desire: Manifesting from Wholeness........................ 89
Wholeness Is Not the Absence of Desire.. 89
The Trap of Chasing Completion Through Creation...................................... 90
Becoming the Source Instead of the Seeker.. 91
Want Less, Become More.. 92

Chapter 16: Self-Sourcing Your Reality.. 94
From Tool Dependency to Inner Mastery.. 94
The Shift from Seeking to Sensing.. 95
Creating from Wholeness, Holding with Power.. 96
You Were Always the Source.. 97

Chapter 17: The 7 Signs You've Shifted Frequencies................................ 101
1. You React Differently to the Same Triggers.. 101
2. You No Longer Chase the Old Timeline... 102
3. Your Inner Dialogue Is Kinder, Clearer, and More Grounded................ 103
4. You Prioritize Alignment Over Outcome... 103
5. You Experience "Clean Wins" That Require Less Effort......................... 104
6. You Attract People Who Reflect Your New Identity................................ 105
7. You Feel Peace Even Without the Proof.. 105
You've Already Shifted—Now Stabilize It.. 106

Chapter 18: Common Mistakes That Kill Manifestations........................ 106
Fear-Based Creation: Manifesting from the Wound, Not the Soul............. 107
Forcing the Outcome: Controlling Instead of Co-Creating......................... 108
Over-Efforting from Misaligned Motivation.. 109
Mistakes Are Just Messages.. 110

Chapter 19: Creating Reality as a Lifestyle, Not a Hack........................... 112
Manifestation as Expression, Not Escape... 112
Consistent Identity Equals Consistent Reality.. 113
Daily Alignment Habits that Sustain Your Frequency................................. 114

Chapter 20: Your Final Unlock: Becoming the Manifestation................. 117
Desire Melts When Identity Matches It.. 117

Your Life Reflects Your Self-Perception.. 118
The End of the Chase Is the Beginning of Real Power... 119
You Are the Destination... 120

You're Manifesting All the Time—But Not Always What You Want

You are manifesting all the time.

Not just when you close your eyes, visualize your dream life, or repeat an affirmation. Every thought you entertain, every emotion you suppress or express, every belief you hold—these are all quietly programming your reality. The question is not if you're manifesting. It's what, why, and from where.

Most people approach manifestation like a performance: they do the morning routine, light the candle, create the vision board, and then wait for the universe to deliver. And sometimes, it works—briefly. But more often, it doesn't. Or it brings partial results, mixed signals, and confusing outcomes that don't reflect the vision they so carefully curated.

That's because there's a hidden layer to manifestation that most teachings skip: the unconscious, emotional, and energetic programming that's beneath your desires. This programming is always active, always broadcasting, and always shaping what shows up in your life.

This book is not about "positive thinking." In fact, that phrase might be doing more harm than good if you're using it to suppress what's real. This book is about the unseen mechanics that drive your ability to create change—not just what you want, but what you actually get.

It's for the people who have been trying—hard—but feel blocked. It's for the ones who sense there's something deeper going on but can't quite name it. It's for the seekers who've read the books, said the affirmations, taken the courses… and still feel like something is missing.

That "something" is what happens beneath your conscious awareness. And until you understand, engage with, and shift the hidden layers of your mind, body, and energy field, your efforts will feel like pushing a boulder uphill.

But here's the good news: when you learn to work with these invisible dynamics, everything changes. Manifestation becomes less about doing and more about being. Less about striving, and more about allowing. The process becomes natural, intuitive, and sustainable.

This book will show you how.

Welcome to Hidden Manifestation—where the magic is in what you don't yet see.

PART I: THE HIDDEN SIDE OF MANIFESTATION

Chapter 1: Why the Surface Techniques Aren't Enough

Manifestation has become mainstream. It's on TikTok, in bookshelves, and on wellness podcasts. Everyone, it seems, is talking about scripting, gratitude lists, and how to raise your vibration. And while there's value in these practices, many people find themselves following the formulas and still not seeing consistent results.

Why?

Because most popular manifestation techniques operate on the surface level. They assume that if you think positively enough, the universe will rearrange itself to match your thoughts. But the reality is more complex.

Your conscious thoughts make up only a small fraction of your total mental and energetic activity. The rest is hidden in your subconscious beliefs, embodied emotional patterns, nervous system responses, and vibrational imprints. When those deeper layers are misaligned with your intentions, no amount of "thinking positive" can override them.

You can create a vision board of your dream house, but if your body is still holding onto scarcity, anxiety, or trauma, that vision remains a fantasy. You might chant affirmations every day, but if your subconscious is rooted in "I'm not worthy," your frequency tells a different story.

The Hidden Conflict Between Conscious Desire and Subconscious Programming

You don't manifest what you say you want—you manifest what you're available for.

That's a hard truth for many, because it suggests that we're unconsciously participating in our disappointments. But it's also empowering, because it means we can change the results by changing the internal conditions.

At any moment, your subconscious is broadcasting a signal. This signal is shaped by past experiences, cultural conditioning, emotional wounds, and nervous system patterns. If you grew up in an environment where money was scarce, love was conditional, or success was dangerous, those imprints are still living inside you.

So even if you consciously want abundance, your subconscious might associate it with fear, responsibility, or even abandonment. And so, without realizing it, you repel the very thing you desire—because part of you doesn't feel safe receiving it. That's why surface techniques often fall flat. They don't reach the places where change actually happens.

Why Willpower Isn't Enough

Many manifestation teachings rely heavily on willpower: think this, feel that, act as if. But willpower is a short-term tool. It's like trying to steer a ship by paddling on the surface while the rudder below pulls you in the opposite direction.

If your internal wiring is not aligned with your desires, you'll either:

- self-sabotage when progress begins,
- attract distorted versions of what you want,
- or manifest in one area while another area crumbles.

This is not because you're broken or "not high-vibe enough." It's because your system—your mind, body, and field—hasn't been updated to match your vision. And that update can't happen through force. It requires safety, awareness, and integration.

The real manifestation work isn't flashy. It's often quiet and deep. It's recognizing when a desire is layered with fear. It's sitting with discomfort instead of avoiding it. It's listening to your body when it tightens in response to success.

When you stop trying to override your inner truth with performance—and start building true coherence between your inner and outer worlds—manifestation becomes magnetic. You become the kind of person to whom results naturally flow.

The Power of Inner Safety and Nervous System Regulation

Here's a truth that few manifestation coaches talk about: your body is the gatekeeper of what you can receive.

You might think you want love, visibility, wealth—but if your nervous system is dysregulated, those things can feel unsafe. And your body will always prioritize survival over success.

That's why people unconsciously push away good opportunities, sabotage relationships, or procrastinate on big moves. Their system is trying to protect them from what it perceives as a threat—even if that "threat" is the very thing they say they want.

Affirmations won't work if your body is in a fight-or-flight state. Visualization won't land if your emotional baseline is distrust. You have to create inner safety first.

That means learning how to down-regulate anxiety, build tolerance for expansion, and recognize the somatic signs of alignment. When your body says "yes," the universe tends to follow.

Time to Go Deeper

Surface-level tools are not wrong—they're simply incomplete. They can help set intention, clarify desire, and shift momentary focus. But they must be accompanied by deeper work if you want lasting change.

In the next Chapters, we'll explore what's really going on beneath your efforts to manifest: the shadow side of intention, the role of the nervous system, and the hidden "static" in your energy field that may be interfering with your frequency.

This is where manifestation becomes not just an act, but a way of being. Because once you align what you want with who you are—from the inside out—nothing stays hidden for long.

Chapter 2: The Shadow Side of Intention

Not all desires are clean.

That may sound strange in a world where setting intentions is considered sacred and desiring more is seen as a sign of alignment. But not all intentions arise from clarity, confidence, or expansion. Many are shaped by fear, lack, or unhealed parts of ourselves. And when that's the case, the very act of intending can contain the seeds of sabotage.

We don't just manifest from what we want—we manifest from who we are being when we want it.

That's the hidden shadow side of intention. It's not that your desires are wrong; it's that they may be unconsciously entangled with emotional residues and energetic distortions. And unless you become aware of those layers, they will shape your outcomes more than the words you speak or the goals you set.

Let's explore this more deeply.

Intentions That Come from Wounds

Many people set intentions from a place of emotional survival, not from soul clarity. They want love because they feel unworthy without it. They want wealth because they're terrified of being dependent. They want success to prove someone wrong, or to finally feel "enough."

These desires often sound powerful on the surface. They can even produce temporary results. But underneath, they carry a wounded frequency—a signal that says, "I'm not whole yet. I need this thing to complete me." And the universe, which reflects your true energetic state more than your spoken affirmations, responds accordingly.

This is why you might attract someone only to feel insecure around them. Or manifest a job that aligns with your goals but drains your soul. The intention pulled something in—but the wound distorted what arrived.

When intentions come from unresolved pain, the manifestation mirrors that pain.

To shift this, you have to ask yourself a deeper question when setting any desire: "Am I wanting this from love or from lack?"

Wanting from love feels expansive, rooted, and stable. It feels like a bonus, not a life raft. Wanting from lack feels anxious, urgent, and conditional. It often comes with fantasies of escape or rescue.

The first builds energy. The second drains it.

Shadow intentions are not bad. But they are invitations—to pause, reflect, and integrate the part of you that believes the manifestation is necessary for your worth. When you heal that, the intention can purify, and what comes in will be cleaner, more sustainable, and more fulfilling.

Energetic Sabotage: When Wanting = Pushing Away

There's a paradox in manifestation: the harder you chase something, the more you signal that you don't have it—and don't believe you can.

This isn't about passivity or pretending not to care. It's about energetic coherence. If your internal state is fixated on the absence of a desire, your intention, no matter how well-worded, becomes a reinforcement of lack.

For example, saying "I want financial freedom" while constantly checking your bank account in fear is not a neutral desire—it's an energetic contradiction. On the surface, you want freedom. But beneath, you're reinforcing the vibration of scarcity every time you seek evidence of its opposite.

This is why you can do all the "right" things—set intentions, visualize outcomes, even take action—and still stay stuck. Because if your actions are laced with desperation, they're not really aligned. They're efforts to force an outcome instead of allowing it to unfold from resonance.

The universe is not responding to your words. It's responding to your frequency. So how do you know if your intention is sabotaging you?

Ask yourself:

- Am I setting this intention with trust or with tension?
- Am I acting from inspiration or fear?
- Do I believe this is possible—or am I trying to prove it against my own doubt?

When you set an intention that is not supported by your deeper energetic state, you create static in your field. That static acts like interference, blurring the signal between you and what you desire.

Energetic sabotage isn't punishment—it's a reflection. It shows you where you're out of alignment. It gives you a chance to go inward and realign, rather than pushing harder from the outside.

When Your Conscious Intention and Subconscious Identity Clash

Let's say you set a powerful intention to be in a loving, secure relationship. You visualize it daily, you journal about it, you even go on dates. But something's off. The people you meet seem unavailable. Or you find yourself pulling away just when things start to get real. Or nothing happens at all.

This isn't because your intention isn't clear. It's because part of you doesn't feel safe being loved in that way.

That's a subconscious identity conflict.

Your conscious mind wants one thing, but your subconscious identity—the inner story you've built about who you are—says something else. Maybe it says, "I'm the one who always has to earn love." Or, "Closeness is dangerous." Or, "I get abandoned when I open up."

So when love approaches, your system either shuts down or attracts someone who will fulfill the old story. The identity wins—every time.

This happens not just in relationships, but with money, health, visibility, and purpose. If you're holding an inner identity of "I'm not good enough," or "I'm not safe with success," or "I always get left behind," your subconscious will override any intention that contradicts it.

This is the most insidious form of manifestation sabotage—because it often happens below awareness. You're not trying to block your desires. But the version of you you're being doesn't yet believe they belong to you.

Here's the key: manifestation requires identity congruence.

Your external results will always match your most dominant internal identity. Not your best intentions, not your positive thoughts—but your felt sense of who you are in the world.

When you shift your identity to match the reality you desire, manifestation accelerates. Not because the universe is rewarding you, but because you've removed the internal resistance that was keeping it at bay.

That shift doesn't happen by pretending or bypassing. It happens through integration—meeting the parts of you that feel scared, small, or unworthy, and bringing them into coherence with the version of you who already has what you want.

Intention Must Be Backed by Integration

Intention is not just a mental exercise. It's a full-spectrum alignment of thought, emotion, energy, and identity.

When you set intentions from clarity, wholeness, and self-trust, they become powerful magnets. But when they come from wounds, fear, or misaligned identities, they can turn into loops of frustration and disappointment.

That's the shadow side of intention: it reveals the parts of us that still feel separate from our desires. But this isn't a flaw—it's a gift. Because once you see the distortion, you can clear it.

The rest of this book will show you how.

You'll learn to regulate your nervous system so it stops rejecting what you're calling in. You'll uncover and shift the subconscious patterns that keep recreating the same unwanted cycles. And you'll begin to live in a way that's congruent with what you desire—not because you're trying harder, but because you're becoming the person who naturally receives it.

The light side of intention is not about effort. It's about alignment.

And that begins with knowing what's hiding in the dark.

Chapter 3: The Nervous System's Role in Manifestation

If your mind sets the goal, your body decides if it's safe to have it.

This is the truth most manifestation teachings overlook. They focus on thoughts, beliefs, and emotions—important elements, yes—but leave out the most primal gatekeeper in the entire system: your nervous system.

The nervous system is not just about stress or relaxation. It's the foundation of your sense of safety in the world. Every choice you make, every opportunity you allow or reject, and every limit you unconsciously uphold is filtered through this deep biological operating system.

You can visualize abundance every morning and repeat affirmations all day, but if your body doesn't feel safe receiving what you're asking for, it will quietly shut the door. And it won't tell you in words. It will tell you through procrastination, avoidance, tension, or unexpected chaos that "proves" you're not ready.

To manifest consistently and sustainably, you must understand and work with your nervous system—not against it.

The Body as a Permission System

At its core, the nervous system is wired for one thing: survival.

It doesn't care about your goals, your vision board, or your intentions. It cares about keeping you alive and away from threat. And the tricky part is that your system often interprets change as threat—even if that change is positive.

Why? Because safety to the nervous system equals familiarity. What you've survived, what you know, what you've repeated over time—this is what your system registers as "safe," even if it's painful or limiting.

So if you've grown up around scarcity, your nervous system is calibrated to expect lack. If your early relationships taught you to anticipate rejection, your system may associate closeness with danger. And if you've learned to minimize yourself to avoid conflict or judgment, visibility can feel unsafe—even when you consciously want to be seen.

This is why manifestations often stall when the stakes feel higher. You start gaining momentum, things begin to shift, and suddenly... sabotage creeps in. You get sick before the big launch. You forget to respond to the opportunity. You pick a fight with your partner just as intimacy deepens.

It's not random. It's regulation.

Your body is trying to return you to what it perceives as safe. Until you retrain it, your nervous system will act as the invisible thermostat of your life—bringing you back to the temperature you've always known.

That's why true manifestation work must include somatic safety. Without it, you're driving with the brakes on.

Fight, Flight, Freeze… or Receive?

Most people are familiar with the stress responses of fight, flight, and freeze. What's less discussed is how these states interact with manifestation.

Each nervous system response generates a different energetic signal—and that signal impacts what you attract, how you respond to opportunities, and how you interpret your reality.

Fight mode might show up as overworking, pushing, hustling to make things happen. You may be trying to manifest success, but your energy is rooted in aggression or hypervigilance. This creates outcomes fueled by force, not flow.

Flight mode often manifests as avoidance, distraction, or perpetual busy-ness. You might want change but unconsciously run from the discomfort of transformation. Opportunities arise, but you're "too overwhelmed" to act on them.

Freeze mode looks like paralysis. You want the manifestation, but feel incapable of taking even the smallest step. You binge information, make endless plans, but never move. Your body is stuck in "don't move—it's dangerous."

None of these states are wrong. They're protective. But they block your receiving channel.

There's another state beyond these: the ventral vagal state, also known as the state of social engagement, connection, and openness. This is where manifestation becomes fluid. Your body is calm, your mind is clear, and your actions are aligned—not rushed or forced. You can hear intuitive nudges. You trust timing. You're responsive, not reactive.

In this state, your system says "yes" to life. And life responds.

To reach this state more often, you must practice nervous system regulation: techniques and habits that teach your body it's safe to expand, safe to receive, and safe to hold more.

Because when your body feels safe, your field opens. And that's when real manifestation begins.

Regulation Before Expansion

One of the biggest mistakes people make in manifestation is trying to leap into a new identity or outcome without preparing the body to hold it.

You can quantum leap, yes—but only to the degree your nervous system can integrate and sustain the shift.

Without regulation, expansion feels threatening. And when something feels threatening, you will unconsciously resist it—no matter how good it sounds.

This is why so many people experience the "rubber band effect": they manifest something big, but can't stabilize it. The money comes in… then disappears. The relationship arrives… then falls apart. The opportunity lands… but they sabotage it.

What's happening here isn't failure. It's a lack of capacity.

Your system hasn't yet developed the capacity to receive and hold the new frequency. And that capacity is built through repeated, embodied experiences of safety.

What does that look like in practice?

It means:

- **Breathing** when you feel overwhelmed, instead of numbing or pushing through.
- **Grounding** before making big decisions.
- **Celebrating** small wins, so your body learns that success isn't dangerous.
- **Resting** when your body asks for it, instead of overriding with hustle.

- **Titrating** change—stretching in small ways rather than leaping into the deep end.

This is the difference between manifesting as an idea and manifesting as a lifestyle. One is fragile. The other is sustainable.

You don't just want to attract what you desire—you want to hold it without collapsing. That's the work of nervous system expansion.

Manifestation Is a Somatic Process

If your nervous system doesn't feel safe, your manifestations will always feel like a chase.

You'll be running toward a vision while your body pulls you back toward the familiar. You'll wonder why things stall, why results disappear, or why everything feels so hard. And you'll think you need more discipline, more affirmations, or better techniques.

But what you really need is safety.

Safety to trust. Safety to receive. Safety to expand beyond your past story.

When your body becomes a place that can hold your desires, manifestation stops being a struggle. It becomes a natural outflow of your alignment. You're no longer forcing change—you're allowing it.

And that's when life begins to meet you, not at the level of your effort, but at the level of your embodiment.

In the next Chapter, we'll dive into another invisible force that affects your manifestation: energetic clutter. Because even with safety and intention, you can't receive clearly if your field is full of static.

But now, you know where it starts: not in your mind, not on your vision board, but in your body.

Your nervous system is your manifestation filter.

Train it well.

Chapter 4: Energetic Clutter: The Hidden Static in Your Field

You can have the clearest intention, the most aligned identity, and a regulated nervous system—but still feel blocked. Still feel like something is off, like your manifestations are delayed, distorted, or oddly inconsistent. When this happens, many people assume they've done something wrong or that they're "out of alignment." But often, the issue isn't with your intention or energy—it's with what's surrounding you.

Enter energetic clutter.

Energetic clutter refers to the unseen noise, interference, and entanglements in your energetic field that dilute your frequency and distort your signal. Just like static can disrupt a radio station, clutter in your field scrambles the clarity of your manifestation. It doesn't mean you're broken or failing. It means your field is carrying more than it's meant to—old thoughts, toxic relationships, outdated commitments, environments that drain instead of support.

You are always broadcasting a signal. That signal isn't just shaped by what's inside you—it's also influenced by what you allow around you.

Let's explore what energetic clutter really is, where it hides, and how to start clearing it to unlock cleaner, faster manifestations.

Thought Loops and Mental Overcrowding

The mind is powerful—but it's also noisy.

One of the most overlooked forms of energetic clutter is obsessive thought. You can be highly spiritual, deeply intentional, and still be living in a loop of anxious forecasting, repetitive inner dialogue, and mental micromanagement of your future.

When you obsess over your manifestation—when it's all you think about, when you keep checking for signs, when you analyze every step and outcome—you're not creating alignment. You're cluttering your signal.

Energetically, this creates the vibration of control and attachment. The message becomes: I don't trust it will happen unless I monitor it constantly. That signal sends confusion into the field. Your mind may be focused, but your energy says, "I'm not sure. I'm scared. I need to interfere."

This kind of mental noise also reduces your capacity to hear intuitive nudges. When your brain is full of "what if"s, "why not yet"s, and "maybe I should"s, your clarity gets drowned in static. You can't receive a message when the channel is crowded.

One of the most powerful things you can do to declutter your mind is learn to let go of mental grasping. That doesn't mean you stop caring. It means you stop chasing the outcome with your thoughts. You focus your mind, release the signal, and return to presence. You drop into your body, into trust, into the moment. Meditation helps. Journaling helps. Even more, space helps—time away from screens, information, and goal-chasing. When you clear mental space, you amplify energetic space. And that makes your manifestation field much more responsive.

Relationships That Distort Your Frequency

Not everyone is meant to come with you into your next Chapter.

This truth is difficult because it touches on one of our deepest needs—connection. But not all connections support your growth. Some entangle your energy. Some drain it. Some reflect old versions of you that you've already outgrown.

People carry energy. And when you are closely bonded to someone, whether through love, obligation, or history, their energy lives in your field. If they are constantly negative, chaotic, or stuck in victimhood, that vibration doesn't stay separate. It pulls on your system. It tugs at your clarity. It feeds your doubt and drags your frequency back to what feels "familiar," not what feels true.

This doesn't mean you cut people out of your life harshly or without compassion. But it does mean you become radically honest about who aligns with your vision—and who doesn't. Who energizes you after a conversation, and who leaves you feeling tight, confused, or small.

Some relationships are rooted in mutual growth. Others are rooted in unspoken contracts that say, "Don't grow, because if you do, I'll feel abandoned." And many of us stay small to avoid that confrontation.

But every time you minimize your light to stay connected, you create friction in your field. You're splitting your signal between expansion and approval, between who you are becoming and who you think others need you to be.

You don't have to hate someone to outgrow them. You can love people and still let go. You can honor the history and still choose your future.

Energetic clutter in relationships often shows up as:

- guilt around saying no
- pressure to maintain an old identity
- constant drama or emotional turbulence
- unspoken resentment or emotional debts
- fear of outshining or losing someone

To manifest clearly, you must become protective of your frequency. That means curating your energetic environment the way an artist curates their tools—with care, clarity, and purpose. Not everyone can walk with you. Not everyone should.

Environmental Noise and Energetic Imprints

Your physical environment holds energy.

This is not just about aesthetics or minimalism. It's about resonance. The objects, spaces, and environments you inhabit either support your frequency—or subtly drain it.

Think about the places where you spend most of your time: your home, your workspace, your car. Do they feel alive, clean, clear, and spacious? Or do they feel stagnant, cluttered, noisy, or emotionally heavy?

Every object holds a story. That gift from someone you no longer speak to? That pile of unread books reminding you of what you "should" do? That corner of your room that hasn't been touched in months? These all create micro-signals. And together, they add up to energetic weight.

When your space is filled with old energy—especially from past versions of yourself—you are unconsciously tethered to timelines that no longer serve you. You're trying to call in a new reality while living in a shrine to the old one.

Clearing your physical space is a form of manifestation magic. Not because it's symbolic (though it is), but because it directly affects your nervous system, your clarity, and your energetic broadcast. When you clean, release, and reconfigure your environment, you send a powerful message to the universe: I am ready to receive something new.

This doesn't mean you need a perfect house or expensive decor. It means you create resonant space—space that feels aligned with your desired state. That could be a single corner of your room that you make sacred. A desk that feels clean and focused. A shelf that holds only what inspires and uplifts you.

If you want a life that feels light, open, and abundant—start by making your space feel that way first. You'd be surprised how quickly the external begins to match.

Protect the Signal

Energetic clutter is not just a nuisance—it's a distortion.

You are an antenna, always sending and receiving. And just like a radio station needs a clear signal to broadcast music, your manifestation requires a clean channel. That means tending to your mental space, your relationships, your physical environment, and even the digital inputs you allow in.

Every podcast, every Instagram account, every conversation—these all affect your frequency. They either clean and sharpen your signal or muddy it.

This is not about becoming paranoid or hyper-controlled. It's about becoming discerning. Knowing what enhances your field and what fogs it. Choosing coherence over chaos. Stillness over stimulation. Alignment over obligation.

When you clear the noise, your true signal becomes unmistakable. And when your signal is strong, the universe doesn't have to guess what you want—it meets you clearly, directly, and consistently.

In the next Chapter, we'll explore how your subconscious programming—especially around money, love, and success—silently shapes what you manifest, and how to start rewriting those hidden scripts. But for now, let this truth sink in:

You don't need to do more to manifest more.

You need to clear more of what's in the way.

Because your desires are already on their way. They just need space to land.

PART II: REWIRING THE INVISIBLE LAYERS

Chapter 5: Subconscious Patterning and Money, Love, Success

Your life is not a reflection of your desires—it's a reflection of your patterns. This is one of the hardest truths to face when it comes to manifestation. We like to believe that what we want is what we move toward. But in reality, we tend to move in circles—repeating the same outcomes, the same frustrations, and the same invisible limits. Why? Because behind every thought, decision, and reaction lies a deeper layer: your subconscious programming.

These are the mental and emotional blueprints formed early in life—imprints from childhood, family systems, cultural narratives, and personal experiences. They sit beneath awareness, running silently in the background. You don't see them. You don't hear them. But they are always shaping what you believe is possible, what you expect, and what you allow.

Subconscious patterning explains why you can desire abundance and still live paycheck to paycheck. Why you can crave love and continue attracting emotionally unavailable people. Why you can dream of success and sabotage yourself every time an opportunity arises.

The good news is: patterns are not destiny. They are conditioning. And what was conditioned can be reconditioned.

Let's explore how these hidden scripts affect the most common areas of manifestation—money, love, and success—and how to begin rewriting them from the inside out.

The Money Blueprint: Scarcity in the Subconscious

Your relationship with money has very little to do with math—and everything to do with memory.

Long before you understood what income, wealth, or prosperity meant, you absorbed emotional cues and unspoken rules from the world around you. These cues became your financial blueprint.

Maybe you grew up in a household where money was always tight, where bills caused tension, or where wealth was talked about with resentment. Maybe you heard things like:

- "We can't afford that."
- "Money doesn't grow on trees."
- "Rich people are greedy."
- "You have to work hard to deserve it."

Each of these phrases, repeated over time, becomes more than a belief. It becomes a truth—a lens through which you see the world and yourself. And no matter how much you want abundance, you'll struggle to receive and keep it if your subconscious associates money with stress, danger, guilt, or unworthiness.

This explains why people who suddenly receive a windfall—through inheritance, lottery, or unexpected success—often lose it quickly. Their inner blueprint doesn't recognize wealth as "safe" or "normal." The subconscious finds a way to bring them back to their energetic baseline.

Rewriting this pattern starts with awareness. Begin noticing the unconscious stories you carry around money. What do you feel when you think about wealth? Expansion—or constriction? Possibility—or fear?

Next, begin building new associations. This isn't about repeating empty affirmations. It's about embodying a different relationship with money:

- Celebrate small financial wins, no matter how minor.
- Learn to hold and manage money without judgment or shame.
- Surround yourself with messages and mentors that normalize abundance.
- Shift from seeing money as power or pressure, to seeing it as support.

When your nervous system and subconscious begin to associate money with freedom, generosity, and peace—you'll stop chasing it. It will begin to flow more naturally into your life, because it no longer threatens your internal world.

The Love Loop: Repeating Emotional Imprints

Love is one of the most desired—and distorted—areas of manifestation. You can want a healthy, secure, passionate partnership. But if the deepest parts of you equate love with abandonment, betrayal, rejection, or control, your subconscious will create situations that reinforce those old dynamics. Not because you want pain—but because pain is familiar. And to the subconscious, familiar equals safe.

This is why people often say, "Why do I keep attracting the same kind of person?" or "Why does every relationship feel like a repeat of the last?" It's not a coincidence. It's a pattern.

These patterns often begin in childhood. The way we attached to caregivers—whether we felt seen, safe, soothed, and secure—becomes the model for how we approach adult intimacy. If love was inconsistent, conditional, or withheld, we may now equate love with anxiety, proving ourselves, or emotional withdrawal.

This creates two major blocks to manifestation in love:

1. You chase emotionally unavailable partners because they mirror what feels normal.
2. You sabotage healthy love because it feels unfamiliar—and therefore threatening.

To shift this, you must begin building emotional safety inside yourself. That means:

- Acknowledging the pain of past relationships without bypassing it.
- Identifying your attachment style and understanding how it plays out in

dating or partnership.
- Practicing nervous system regulation in moments of connection, so you don't shut down or over-activate.
- Most of all, learning to source love internally—not as a substitute for connection, but as the foundation for it.

When you stop making love a reward for worthiness and start experiencing it as a natural expression of who you are, your field changes. You stop chasing. You start magnetizing. You begin calling in partners who match your healed self—not your old wounds.

The Success Pattern: Identity, Worth, and Self-Concept

Success is not just about action—it's about identity.

You can have all the strategies, goals, and ambition in the world. But if your subconscious doesn't believe you're someone who succeeds—who finishes, who rises, who deserves to be seen—you'll unconsciously block the results you claim to want.

This pattern often shows up as:
- Procrastination, disguised as "perfectionism"
- Downplaying your achievements
- Avoiding visibility
- Picking fights with authority or sabotaging momentum just before a breakthrough

At the root is a question many of us avoid asking: Who am I when I succeed? Success isn't just about achieving something. It's about becoming someone new. And that shift in identity can feel threatening if your current self-concept is rooted in struggle, failure, or invisibility.

Maybe being successful feels like a betrayal of your family system. Maybe it triggers fears of being judged or envied. Maybe deep down, you believe that to be loved, you must be small.

To change this, you don't need to force a new identity—you need to gently expand your capacity to hold a new one. That starts with re-patterning your self-concept:

- Begin noticing where you downplay yourself. Then, stop.
- Let people see your gifts—even when it makes you nervous.
- Take small risks that stretch your sense of what's possible.
- Surround yourself with people who reflect the future version of you, not just the familiar one.

When your internal story about who you are matches the reality you want to create, success becomes sustainable. You're not performing it. You're living it.

Awareness Is the First Alchemy

Subconscious patterning is not your fault—but it is your responsibility.

These patterns were installed without your consent. But now, you have the power to change them. And manifestation, at its most honest level, is the process of becoming aware of your patterns, choosing new ones, and aligning your inner world with what you want to see in the outer.

There is no magic affirmation that overrides subconscious sabotage. There is only presence, patience, and the decision to rewire your reality—one thought, one belief, one emotional shift at a time.

As you continue through this book, you'll learn how to access deeper layers of your emotional and energetic self, how to shift vibration in ways that go beyond mood, and how to live in alignment with your future self now—not someday.

But remember this: your patterns are not permanent. They are permissions. They either permit you to rise—or to repeat.

And you are the one who gets to rewrite them.

Chapter 6: Emotional Encoding: What You Feel Is What You Call In

Manifestation doesn't respond to what you say. It responds to what you feel. This is a fundamental truth that many overlook, especially when trapped in the world of mental manifestation—affirmations, scripting, vision boards, mindset hacks. These can all be helpful tools, but they operate primarily at the level of thought. And thought, while powerful, is not the deepest language of the universe.

Emotion is.

Emotion is energy in motion. It is the vibrational signature you carry into every moment, and it encodes the messages you send out into the quantum field. If thoughts are the blueprint, emotion is the electricity. If vision is the seed, emotion is the soil in which it grows.

But not all emotion is conscious. In fact, most people are carrying emotional encoding that was set years ago—encoding rooted in trauma, repetition, and unconscious association. These hidden emotions shape the frequency you transmit to the world. And more than anything else, that frequency determines what you attract.

To become a powerful, clear, and aligned creator, you must understand what you are emotionally broadcasting—often beneath your awareness—and how to shift it without forcing or faking positivity.

The Hidden Code Beneath Your Desires

Every desire carries an emotional charge. You don't just want money—you want the feeling of freedom, security, or expansion that you believe it will bring. You don't just want love—you want connection, belonging, or adoration. Every vision is, at its core, a container for an emotion you crave.

This is why emotional clarity is so essential. When your emotional state is aligned with the frequency of what you desire, manifestation becomes smoother and more magnetic. But when the emotion you hold contradicts the feeling of the outcome you seek, you create friction.

For example, if you want a successful career but feel consistently anxious, unseen, or overwhelmed, your emotional field is not in resonance with success—it's in resonance with stress. If you want love but are carrying a deep well of fear, resentment, or shame, that becomes the emotional signature you emit—even if your words say otherwise.

This disconnect between desire and emotional reality is one of the biggest blocks in manifestation. It's also why you can "want" something intensely and not manifest it—because the desire is being transmitted with a contradictory frequency.

The solution is not to suppress or override your current emotions with forced joy or fake positivity. That only deepens the split within you. Instead, you must integrate your emotional reality, understand what it's trying to tell you, and consciously cultivate the emotional states that match your intended outcomes. This isn't about ignoring what's real. It's about becoming emotionally sovereign.

Emotional Repetition Creates Reality

The universe listens less to what you feel once and more to what you feel repeatedly.

Your dominant emotional state—your habitual emotional baseline—is what truly writes your reality. A single moment of joy or gratitude is powerful, but unless it becomes part of your energetic norm, it won't have the gravity to pull consistent results into your life.

Emotional encoding is created through repetition. Think of it like a radio station:

the longer you stay tuned to a certain frequency, the clearer and stronger that signal becomes. If you've been in states of disappointment, frustration, or hopelessness for months or years, those frequencies have been reinforced. They're not just moods—they've become energetic defaults.

But defaults can be changed.

The first step is awareness. Begin to notice your most frequent emotional states. Not just the ones you perform for others, but the ones you return to when no one's watching. Do you often feel rushed? Powerless? Tense? Lonely? These emotional states are shaping what you expect, what you tolerate, and what you magnetize.

The next step is intentional emotional practice. This doesn't mean pretending. It means practicing the emotional frequency of your desired life—even before it arrives.

For example, if your dream reality includes a sense of peace and abundance, ask yourself: how can I practice the feeling of peace today, even in small ways? Can I give myself five minutes of stillness without my phone? Can I breathe more slowly, or create an environment that soothes my nervous system?

If your future self feels powerful and fulfilled, how can you engage with your day from that energy? Can you walk with a bit more intention? Can you speak more clearly? Can you make one decision from trust instead of fear?

Small shifts in emotional state, practiced consistently, rewire your energetic field. They become your new baseline. And when the baseline changes, your reality does too.

The Danger of Emotional Bypassing

In the personal development and manifestation space, there's often pressure to "stay high vibe," to think happy thoughts, and to focus only on the positive.

While intention and focus do matter, this mindset can lead to one of the most harmful habits in spiritual work: emotional bypassing.

Emotional bypassing is the act of suppressing or ignoring your real emotional experiences in order to appear "spiritually evolved" or energetically clean. It's the tendency to judge fear, sadness, anger, or grief as "low vibe" and therefore unacceptable.

But here's the truth: emotion, in and of itself, is not good or bad. It's information. It's energy. And every emotion you experience—even the painful ones—carries a message, a need, or a wound that wants to be seen.

When you bypass your emotions in the name of manifestation, you split yourself. You create a false self that smiles while the real you contracts. You send mixed signals into the field: one of forced positivity and one of repressed pain. This not only clutters your vibration—it exhausts you.

True emotional power doesn't come from controlling your feelings. It comes from meeting them. From learning to be with sadness without drowning in it. To feel anger without becoming reactive. To hold grief without collapsing.

This level of emotional maturity sends a much cleaner signal. It says, "I trust myself to feel. I am safe in my own energy. I don't need to fake it to attract it." And ironically, the more you allow yourself to feel authentically, the more naturally you begin to shift into higher states—because nothing is being suppressed. You begin to move emotions through the body, not store them. You stop clinging to pain, and you stop chasing happiness. You simply are, and that authenticity becomes magnetic.

Emotion Is the Bridge Between Inner and Outer

If your manifestations feel delayed, distorted, or distant, start by asking: what am I consistently feeling about this desire?

Am I feeling hopeful—or doubtful? Am I feeling inspired—or desperate? Am I practicing gratitude—or focusing on lack? Your emotions don't need to be perfect. They need to be honest. And then they need to be chosen with care. Emotion is the bridge between the invisible and the visible. It is the current that carries your intentions into form. You are not required to feel happy all the time to manifest powerfully. But you are required to know your emotions—and to choose, when you can, the ones that reflect your true alignment.

In the next Chapter, we'll explore how your identity shapes your manifestations—and how becoming the person who already has what you desire is one of the most powerful frequency shifts available. But for now, remember:

You are not creating from your thoughts alone.

You are creating from the emotional code you carry.

And that code is yours to rewrite.

Chapter 7: Identity Alchemy: Be the One Who Has It

Manifestation is not about getting what you want. It's about becoming who you are when you already have it.

This shift—from "how do I get it" to "who am I when I live it"—is the heart of identity alchemy. Until now, we've talked about subconscious programming, emotional encoding, and energetic alignment. But beneath all of that lies something even more fundamental: your sense of self.

Your identity is your energetic container. It defines what you believe is possible, what you feel worthy of, what you think is "you" and "not you." You can only hold in your life what your identity can accommodate. Everything else bounces off, falls apart, or feels like an accident.

To manifest lasting change, you must upgrade not just your actions, not just your feelings—but your identity structure. That means dissolving the version of yourself who survived your past and stepping into the version of yourself who lives your future.

You don't manifest from what you hope for. You manifest from what you embody. And embodiment begins with becoming the version of you who already lives in the reality you desire.

Self-Concept: The Silent Governor of Reality

Your self-concept is the most powerful, least visible force in your life.

It's not just how you see yourself—it's how you expect yourself to be. It includes your inner assumptions, your energetic posture, your reflexive choices, and your emotional baseline. It's the story you've been telling yourself about who you are. For example, if you see yourself as "someone who always struggles," you will unconsciously filter reality to support that narrative. Even when ease is available, you'll either overlook it, push it away, or feel guilty for receiving it. If your identity includes the belief "I'm not good at relationships," you'll show up with that expectation, and attract or create dynamics that confirm it.

Most self-concepts were not chosen. They were inherited or conditioned. You may carry the beliefs of your family, culture, peer group, or past self. These beliefs form your "normal," and you unconsciously organize your life to stay within their boundaries.

This is why change can feel so hard, even when you want it. You're trying to bring in a new reality with an outdated self-concept. You want abundance, but still see yourself as broke. You want to be loved, but still feel unworthy. You want visibility, but still identify as the person who stays behind the scenes.

To shift your life, you must shift the lens through which you experience yourself. Start asking: Who do I believe I am? What kind of person do I see myself as—financially, emotionally, creatively? Do I see myself as powerful or passive? Magnetic or invisible? Do I walk into a room expecting to be received—or rejected?

Until you upgrade your self-concept, new results will feel foreign. And what feels foreign can't stay. Identity alchemy means choosing a new "normal" for who you are—and then living from it, even before the world reflects it back.

Embodying the Future Self in the Present Moment

One of the most effective ways to shift identity is through the practice of embodied future selfing. This means getting clear on who you would be—how you'd think, feel, move, speak, and choose—if the manifestation had already occurred. Then, instead of waiting for it to happen, you begin to live as that person now.

This is not about faking or pretending. It's not about tricking the universe. It's about activating a new frequency within yourself by becoming a vibrational match for the reality you desire.

Your brain and nervous system don't distinguish much between memory, imagination, and experience. When you consistently align with the emotions, choices, and identity of your future self, your inner world begins to rewire. The body adjusts. The emotions stabilize. The field shifts.

Here's how to begin:

- Ask yourself: If I already had what I want, how would I feel in my body today?
- What would I no longer tolerate?
- How would I respond to challenges?
- What would I choose differently, not out of fear, but from trust?

Then practice that. Not perfectly, not forcefully—but consistently. Choose one small way each day to act in alignment with your future self. Maybe it's how you handle your money, how you set a boundary, or how you take care of your body. These micro-embodiments send a message to your subconscious: "This is who we are now." And as that message repeats, your identity begins to shift—not just mentally, but energetically.

Eventually, the world doesn't change because you fought harder. It changes because you became someone new—and the world had to meet you there.

Letting Go of the Identity That's Attached to the Old Story

To become someone new, you must release who you were when you needed to survive.

This is the part of identity alchemy most people resist. We hold onto old identities because they're familiar—even if they're painful. We cling to the role of the underdog, the outsider, the misunderstood, the self-sacrificing one. These identities may have kept us safe, connected, or validated in the past. But they also become prisons.

You can't step into your expanded life while still committed to your wounded identity.

Ask yourself:

- What parts of my current identity feel safe, but small?
- Who do I keep being because it's familiar, not because it's true?
- What story about myself am I willing to retire?

Letting go of an identity can feel like grief. You might feel disoriented, unmoored, even lonely. That's normal. You're stepping out of a known pattern, and the ego often interprets that as danger. But that discomfort is a sign of growth. It means you're no longer running your life from survival.

Your new identity won't be a costume. It will be a home. A place where your vision doesn't feel far away—it feels lived, expressed, and natural. Where you don't have to reach for your desires—they rise up from within you.

And the more you commit to this version of yourself, the more your outer world reorganizes to match. Opportunities appear. Relationships shift. Synchronicities unfold. Not because you chased them—but because you became someone who receives them.

Identity Is the Root Frequency

You are not manifesting from your effort. You are manifesting from your essence.

That essence is shaped by identity—not just who you think you are, but who you're being, moment to moment. If you've been doing all the right things and still not seeing results, don't push harder. Go deeper. Ask: Am I being the person who already lives this life—or am I trying to earn it from a place of lack?

Manifestation is not a reward for good behavior. It is a reflection of energetic coherence. And when your identity is aligned with your desire, there is no resistance. No forcing. Just matching.

So let this be your invitation: stop waiting to become who you already are. Stop waiting for the outside world to confirm what you know inside. Choose your identity first. Anchor it with practice. Stabilize it with action. And let the world rise to meet you.

In the next Chapter, we'll explore how to truly understand your vibration—not just as emotion, but as a measurable, malleable frequency. Because once your identity is clear, your vibration becomes your amplifier. And the universe is always listening.

Chapter 8: Vibration ≠ Emotion: The True Frequency Formula

It's common to hear that your vibration creates your reality. While this is true, the word "vibration" is often misunderstood, oversimplified, or reduced to emotional states. You may have been told to "stay high vibe" or "raise your vibration" by focusing on joy, gratitude, or excitement—but these instructions, while well-meaning, can create confusion, shame, and disconnection if not deeply understood.

Vibration is not just how you feel in the moment. It's not a mood. It's not a fleeting emotion. Your vibration is a composite of your energetic signal over time—a blend of your dominant thoughts, emotions, body state, identity, and subconscious beliefs. It is a deeper frequency than temporary emotion. It includes your nervous system regulation, the level of safety you feel in receiving, and the degree of alignment between who you are and what you're calling in. This Chapter will guide you in separating temporary emotions from true vibration, teach you how to measure your alignment with more accuracy, and show you how to shift and stabilize your frequency without bypassing or forcing positivity.

Your Vibration Is a Composite Signal

Imagine your vibration as a radio frequency. When you're tuned to a station, you don't just hear one note—you hear a song, a tone, a collection of sounds that form a whole. In the same way, your vibration is the sum of many signals you're sending out all at once.

This includes:
- Your core emotional state
- Your habitual thoughts and inner dialogue
- Your body's sense of safety or threat

- Your self-concept and identity
- Your energetic boundaries and openness
- The clarity (or clutter) of your environment

It's not one feeling that defines your vibration, but the overall pattern. You might have a moment of frustration or sadness, but still be vibrationally aligned with abundance if your baseline frequency is one of trust, worthiness, and inner safety. Conversely, you could be in a good mood but vibrating in scarcity if your core belief is that you're unsupported or lacking.

This is why emotional spikes—temporary highs from visualizations or affirmations—don't always lead to lasting results. They might feel good in the moment, but if they're not rooted in deeper belief and regulation, they dissipate quickly and don't leave a stable imprint in your field.

Your true vibration is what your system returns to when you're not trying to perform, force, or control. It's the energetic posture you hold most of the time. And it's what the universe responds to.

To understand your vibration, start asking: What is the emotional and energetic theme of my life lately? Not just in one moment, but as a pattern over the past days, weeks, or months? That's your frequency—not the emotion you post on social media, but the truth you carry inside.

How to Measure Alignment (Beyond How You Feel)

Because vibration is deeper than emotion, it requires more than mood-tracking to assess. You can't rely solely on "feeling good" as your compass. Sometimes growth is uncomfortable. Sometimes alignment feels quiet or unfamiliar, not exciting or euphoric. This means you need more nuanced ways to measure whether you're in vibrational alignment with what you're manifesting.

Here are some practical indicators:

1. **Inner Congruence**

    Congruence is when your thoughts, feelings, and actions all line up. You say yes and you mean yes. You make a decision and your body relaxes. You think about your future and feel peace, not pressure. This kind of inner alignment creates a coherent frequency that others can feel and the universe can respond to.

2. **Energetic Cleanliness**

    When your vibration is aligned, you feel lighter—not necessarily "happy," but unburdened. There's less noise in your system. You're not overanalyzing, second-guessing, or trying to force outcomes. You're not over-attached to signs or symptoms. You feel clear. You trust your own timing.

3. **Feedback from the Environment**

    Alignment doesn't always mean immediate results—but it often produces resonance. People respond to you differently. Opportunities feel smoother. Synchronicities appear. If your outer world begins reflecting the energy of your inner world more often, that's a good sign your vibration is shifting.

4. **Emotional Neutrality or Grounded Excitement**

    Contrary to what some believe, the most aligned vibrational states are often not euphoric. They're grounded, clear, and steady. You may feel inspired, but not manic. Calm, but not flat. There's a quiet confidence rather than a need to prove. This is a sign you're inhabiting the vibration of having—not chasing.

5. **Resilience and Recovery**

    Being in alignment doesn't mean you never get triggered. It means you recover faster. You notice when you've veered off and gently come back to center. You stop dramatizing your setbacks. You stop making temporary emotions mean permanent failure. You ride the wave instead of resisting it.

Vibrational alignment, then, is not a perfect state. It's a living, dynamic process of coming back to yourself, again and again, until that state becomes your home.

Stabilizing Your Frequency Without Bypassing

Once you begin to understand your vibration, the next step is learning how to shift and stabilize it—without bypassing your actual emotional experience. This is crucial, because trying to "force high vibe" through denial or suppression only creates more static in your field.

Stabilization doesn't mean locking yourself into one emotional state. It means creating an internal environment where your dominant signal is clear, calm, and coherent—even when life is messy.

Here are some grounded ways to support vibrational stability:

1. **Regulate Before You Elevate**

    If your nervous system is dysregulated, you cannot access aligned vibration. Period. Before trying to raise your vibration, take time to ground, breathe, and calm your body. Practices like deep breathing, walking in nature, EFT tapping, or somatic awareness work better than forced affirmations when you're in a reactive state.

2. **Titrate Your Expansion**

    You don't have to leap from fear to joy. That often causes more distress. Instead, shift your vibration gently. Ask: What feels slightly better right now? Move from fear to curiosity, from doubt to openness, from tension to awareness. These small steps create real shifts that your body can integrate.

3. **Anchor New Emotional States Through Action**

    Vibration stabilizes through embodiment. If you want to anchor the vibration of abundance, make decisions from abundance—even in small ways. If you want to stabilize love, express it through words and actions. Identity, emotion, and behavior reinforce one another. Use action to lock in new frequencies.

4. **Create Vibrational Rituals**

    Daily rituals don't have to be elaborate. A 10-minute morning check-in. A song that gets you into alignment. A journaling practice to tune into your future self. These practices work not because they're magical, but because they create consistency—and consistency creates coherence.

5. **Clean Your Field**

    Notice what throws off your vibration. Is it certain people? Social media? Clutter? Energy vampires? These external factors matter. Your frequency is affected by what you allow in your space. Protect your field with intention, boundaries, and regular energetic hygiene.

As you stabilize your frequency, you'll begin to notice something: you're no longer manifesting from hope or urgency. You're simply expressing what's already inside. Manifestation becomes a mirror, not a mystery.

Feel It, But Know What You're Really Feeling

The phrase "raise your vibration" is incomplete without depth. True vibrational alignment is not about chasing a mood. It's about creating a coherent, stable, and embodied frequency that matches the reality you want to live in.

That requires more than momentary emotions. It requires identity shifts, nervous system regulation, emotional intelligence, and energetic hygiene. But most of all, it requires honesty—being honest about what you're really feeling, what your system is truly holding, and what you're broadcasting when no one's watching. When you understand vibration as a full-spectrum frequency—beyond emotion—you unlock the most powerful dimension of manifestation.

In the next Chapter, we'll enter the mechanics of action: how to move from feeling to clarity to movement, and how to use your energy wisely to collapse timelines. Because when your vibration is clean, aligned action becomes inevitable—and that's where real momentum lives.

PART III: THE DEEP ALIGNMENT METHOD

Chapter 9: The 3-Phase Manifestation Flow: Feel → Clear → Act

Manifestation is not a one-time ritual. It is not a list of steps to follow and then wait. It is a living, breathing process—an energetic loop that repeats and refines as you evolve. Many people approach manifestation as if it were a linear journey: set a goal, do some mindset work, visualize, and wait for results. But reality creation doesn't work in straight lines. It works in spirals, cycles, and feedback loops.

When you understand the energetic rhythm behind manifestation, you stop forcing outcomes and start working with the natural current of creation. This current flows through three essential stages: **Feel**, **Clear**, and **Act**.

These are not rigid stages to be checked off like a to-do list. They are energetic states that repeat and deepen. You may pass through all three in a single day or over weeks. You may revisit one multiple times as new layers emerge. But when these three elements are honored and practiced, manifestation stops being a hopeful exercise and becomes a grounded, intuitive art.

Feel: Aligning With the Emotional Blueprint

Every manifestation begins with emotion—whether you realize it or not. Even the most detailed vision board or journal entry is simply a container for a feeling you want to experience. The house, the relationship, the money, the success—they are all symbols of an emotional frequency you are seeking to embody.

To begin the flow, you must first identify and connect with the core feeling of your desire. This goes deeper than "I want more money." Ask yourself: what does having more money represent for me? Is it freedom? Safety? Power? Generosity?

The emotion is the true destination, and the external result is merely one possible path to get there.

Once you've identified the emotion, the next step is to practice it now. This is not about pretending or faking. It's about allowing your system to taste the feeling, even in small, grounded ways. If you want to feel freedom, where can you give yourself more space today? If you want to feel love, how can you offer connection to yourself or someone else without waiting?

The more you feel the desired state in the present moment, the more your nervous system normalizes it, and the more magnetic you become. This is not a spiritual trick—it's biology. Your brain begins to wire for the new reality. Your field shifts. You stop chasing, and you begin receiving from a space of resonance.

But this feeling stage also requires honesty. If you struggle to access the desired state—if it feels fake, forced, or unavailable—there is something in the way. That's where the next phase comes in.

Clear: Releasing the Static and Resistance

Once you've identified the feeling you want to embody, the second step is to clear whatever is preventing you from accessing it fully. This is where most people get stuck—because this phase is often uncomfortable. It brings to the surface the parts of you that don't yet feel safe having what you want.

Resistance is not a sign that you're failing. It's a sign that you're close to change. The nervous system is surfacing old beliefs, emotions, and identities that are misaligned with your intention, so you can meet them, feel them, and release them.

Clearing can look like:
- Emotional processing: letting yourself cry, grieve, rage, or feel through the emotions that have been suppressed around your desire.

- Pattern recognition: noticing when old beliefs or fears arise, such as "I'm not worthy," "This always goes wrong," or "Who am I to want this?"
- Energetic detox: removing people, environments, habits, or information that reinforce your old identity and block your frequency.

Clearing is about making space. You cannot pour clean water into a muddy glass without first emptying what's inside. And most people are trying to manifest on top of emotional residue, trauma imprints, and limiting beliefs. That's why their efforts feel heavy, confusing, or ineffective.

The key to this phase is compassion. Do not judge what arises. Do not try to fix it with another affirmation or productivity hack. Instead, be willing to pause. To listen. To feel. To be with the part of you that doesn't yet believe the manifestation is safe or possible.

When you meet resistance with presence instead of pressure, it begins to dissolve. Not because you "fixed" it, but because you stopped fighting it. That creates energetic flow. And from that cleared space, your next move becomes obvious.

Act: Moving From Alignment, Not Anxiety

After feeling and clearing, you are primed for aligned action.

This is where many manifestation teachings either go too far or not far enough. Some say action is everything—you have to hustle, grind, and force your way to results. Others say action isn't necessary at all, that the universe will deliver everything if you just stay in alignment.

The truth is in the integration. Aligned action is not about effort or intensity. It's about taking the next step that matches your frequency. It's not about doing more—it's about doing what is true.

Aligned action is the physical expression of your energetic state. It confirms your new identity. It tells the universe, "I'm ready," not just in thought but in motion. You'll know action is aligned when:

- It feels like a natural next step, not a forced obligation.
- It comes with a sense of calm, not panic.
- It moves you forward, even if just one inch, and opens space for momentum.
- It's often small, ordinary, and surprisingly easy.

For example, if you've cleared fear around visibility and are stepping into the vibration of leadership, your aligned action might be publishing a blog post, speaking up in a meeting, or creating something new. If you've shifted into a frequency of abundance, your action might be opening a new savings account, making a generous gesture, or saying no to something that feels like scarcity. Sometimes the action will be bold. Sometimes it will be subtle. The point is not what you do—it's why you're doing it. Aligned action flows from clarity, not urgency. From intuition, not anxiety.

And each time you act from alignment, you strengthen the loop. You feel more. You clear more. You act more. The process accelerates, because your energy is no longer fragmented. You become coherent—and coherence is irresistible.

Rinse and Repeat, Again and Again

The manifestation flow is not something you do once. It's a rhythm you live. Feel → Clear → Act. Again and again. With each cycle, you refine. You deepen. You become more of who you truly are, and your outer world reflects that back with increasing clarity.

This process honors both the energetic and the practical. It invites you to slow down and feel, to meet your inner blocks with honesty, and to move through life with intention. It's not about controlling outcomes. It's about becoming the version of you who effortlessly calls them in.

There will be days when you feel stuck, and that's okay. That's part of the clearing. There will be moments when action feels hard, and that's okay, too. Trust the loop. Trust the rhythm. Trust yourself.

In the next Chapter, we'll dive deeper into the micro-decisions that accelerate this process—tiny choices made from alignment that collapse timelines and create rapid transformation. But for now, remember this:

You don't have to chase your desires.

You have to become their match.

And this flow—Feel, Clear, Act—is how you do it.

Chapter 10: The Power of Micro-Decisions

Big change doesn't come from big leaps. It comes from tiny, often overlooked, consistent decisions—the ones you make moment by moment, often without realizing their impact. These are your micro-decisions. And while they may seem small on the surface, they hold the power to bend time, collapse old timelines, and initiate massive transformation.

Micro-decisions are the subtle but critical choices you make daily. Whether to speak kindly to yourself in your inner dialogue. Whether to follow an intuitive nudge instead of defaulting to fear. Whether to close the laptop and rest instead of pushing through. Each of these choices reflects the version of you you are choosing to be—and, therefore, the future you are aligning with.

In manifestation, we tend to overemphasize peak experiences and dramatic shifts. We crave the big moment when everything changes. But the universe often moves in whispers, not shouts. And your frequency is not defined by what you do once in a while, but by the energetic tone you set repeatedly through these micro-decisions.

If you want to accelerate your manifestation, focus less on the finish line and more on the frequency of each step. The compound effect of aligned micro-decisions will get you there faster than any dramatic overhaul ever could.

Your Life Is Built on Invisible Choices

Every day, from the moment you wake up, you're making hundreds of decisions. Most of them are unconscious—habitual reactions based on old programming. What you think about in the shower. What tone you use to speak to yourself. Whether you pause to breathe or jump into stress. Whether you scroll mindlessly or move with intention.

These tiny choices build momentum. And momentum is magnetic. When your micro-decisions align with the identity and frequency of your desired future, you create a coherent energetic field. That coherence signals to the universe: this isn't just a wish—it's a lived frequency.

Most people underestimate the power of these moments because they don't bring instant gratification. But manifestation isn't magic—it's momentum. And that momentum is fueled by choice.

Ask yourself:

- Who am I choosing to be in this moment?
- Is this choice reflecting my old self or my future self?
- What is the smallest shift I can make right now that aligns me with what I want to call in?

Even something as simple as how you respond to an email, how you greet your partner, or how you eat your lunch can carry a vibrational signature. When done with intention, the ordinary becomes sacred. And the sacred becomes a portal for transformation.

You don't need to change your whole life in a day. You need to choose your future one moment at a time.

Decision Fatigue vs. Decision Precision

One of the reasons people struggle with manifestation is that they live in a state of constant decision fatigue. They're overwhelmed by choices, options, and what-if scenarios. The mental load of daily life leaves little space for intentional creation.

This is why clarity and precision in micro-decisions are so important. Precision doesn't mean perfection—it means presence. When you are present with each choice, you reduce energetic leakage. You stop wasting energy on indecision, self-doubt, and reactivity. You begin to move from clarity instead of chaos.

The key to decision precision is anchoring in your future identity. That version of you—the one who has what you want—is not confused about who they are. They may not know every step, but they make decisions from a place of alignment, not fear.

You can begin practicing this by creating what's known as a "decision anchor." This is a simple reference point that reminds you of your future self's priorities. For example:

- "I'm the kind of person who chooses calm over urgency."
- "I take care of my energy before I take care of my to-do list."
- "I move like someone who trusts their timing."

When you feel overwhelmed, pause and ask: What would this version of me do right now? Then take that step—even if it feels small or insignificant.

By building a habit of precision through presence, you reduce friction. Life becomes smoother. You stop second-guessing yourself. You stop outsourcing your power. And every micro-decision becomes a statement of identity, a vote for the timeline you're walking into.

Tiny Acts That Collapse Time

The most surprising thing about micro-decisions is how they collapse time. When you consistently act in alignment with your future self, results that once seemed distant begin to arrive faster—not because you forced them, but because you aligned with the frequency where they already exist.

Time is not just linear. It's elastic, especially in the realm of energy and intention. When you act from your past, you repeat timelines. When you act from your future, you collapse them.

Let's say you're manifesting a new level of abundance. You may think you need to change jobs, find a mentor, or build a new strategy. And while those things matter, they usually don't begin there. The shift starts when you begin acting like someone who values and respects money today. That might mean cleaning up your finances, blessing what you already have, or saying no to scarcity-based decisions. These micro-acts create a ripple that collapses the time between where you are and where you're going.

Or maybe you want a deep, loving relationship. You don't have to wait for someone to show up to start acting like someone who is loved. You can begin by being present with yourself, expressing affection freely, setting clear boundaries, and surrounding yourself with people who reflect healthy love. Those choices are a match for your vision. And when your life is already vibrating at the frequency of love, love finds you faster.

You may not always see the results instantly, but the shift happens immediately. Because the moment you make a decision that aligns with your future, the energy around you begins to rearrange.

The choice is the catalyst. The follow-through is the bridge.

Aligning the Ordinary with the Extraordinary

Manifestation isn't about controlling the universe. It's about mastering your own energy. And the most effective way to master your energy is to pay attention to the seemingly small moments—your micro-decisions.

These are the moments that no one else sees, the ones that don't go on your vision board or your highlight reel. But they are where your future is being shaped.

You don't have to wait for a breakthrough. You are already making one with every choice you make that aligns with who you are becoming.

So take the pressure off needing to know every step. Focus instead on showing up in alignment now. Make decisions that reflect where you're going, not where you've been. And trust that the power of your frequency, expressed consistently in the ordinary, will lead to the extraordinary.

In the next Chapter, we'll explore how to recognize when your manifestation is working—even if there's no visible proof yet. Because sometimes, the most powerful confirmation isn't the result—it's the shift in how you move through the world. And if your micro-decisions are changing, your reality is already catching up.

Chapter 11: How to Know If It's Working (Even When It Looks Like It's Not)

One of the most disorienting aspects of manifestation is the stretch between intention and outcome. You set the desire, align your energy, feel the shift… and then nothing seems to happen. You look around and see the same circumstances, the same bank balance, the same relationship status, the same feedback loop. Doubt creeps in. Did I do something wrong? Am I not "high vibe" enough? Is it even working?

This Chapter is here to remind you that manifestation is often silent before it's visible. It's energetic long before it's material. Just because you don't see immediate proof doesn't mean your field isn't already rearranging. In fact, the absence of results is often the exact space where the deepest transformation is occurring—beneath the surface.

There are signs, though. Subtle, powerful indicators that your manifestation is not only working, but anchoring into reality. These signs are not always external, and they may not look like progress in a traditional sense. But when you learn to recognize them, you stop needing proof to feel certain. You begin to trust the inner shifts as much as the outer ones. And in that trust, things accelerate.

Shifts in Your Inner Landscape

Before a manifestation arrives, your internal world begins to change. Your thoughts feel different. Your emotional baseline begins to move. You start responding to life in new ways—even before your life actually changes.

One of the first signs that things are working is a growing sense of detachment from the outcome. Not because you've given up, but because you're no longer gripping the result as your only source of fulfillment. You've started to embody the emotional frequency of what you desire, and that internal embodiment makes you less needy, less anxious, and more centered.

You may also notice a quiet confidence replacing old patterns of doubt. You're not performing trust anymore—you actually feel it. It's subtle. It's not about shouting affirmations or "acting as if." It's a still, grounded knowing that you are becoming the person who lives this reality, even if the world hasn't caught up yet. Another key indicator is how you relate to your past. When your manifestation is working, you stop being emotionally entangled with old stories. The wounds lose their charge. You begin to remember painful experiences with more neutrality or even gratitude. This doesn't mean bypassing—it means that your energy is no longer stuck in repetition. You're integrating. You're reclaiming space for something new.

Watch for these signs:

- You're less reactive to triggers that once consumed you.
- You feel more ease in letting go of what doesn't serve.
- You make decisions that reflect your future, not your past.
- You catch yourself thinking, "I don't know why, but I just feel different."

That inner difference is not imagination. It's frequency. And frequency always leads.

Subtle Real-World Feedback

Even when the big outcome hasn't arrived, the world around you begins to reflect your shift in small but meaningful ways. These moments are easy to overlook if you're only focused on the final goal. But they are signs that your manifestation is taking root.

One sign is an increase in synchronicities. You start seeing repeating numbers, overhearing conversations that mirror your thoughts, stumbling upon resources or ideas that support your next step. These are not random. They're feedback from the field, showing you that your inner world is resonating with a new timeline.

You may also notice a change in the people around you. Old connections might fall away without drama. New people enter your life who reflect your evolving energy. Conversations become more aligned. Opportunities that once felt out of reach begin to show up in casual, unexpected ways.

Another subtle signal is clarity. You suddenly know what to do—even if it's not what you expected. The fog lifts. The path ahead may not be fully visible, but the next step becomes obvious. You no longer overthink every move because your inner compass is stronger.

It's important here to stay attuned without becoming obsessive. If you're constantly looking for signs to prove your manifestation is working, you're still operating from lack. But if you can witness these moments with calm curiosity, they become fuel—not crutches.

Progress may look like:

- Receiving compliments or feedback that affirm your growth.
- Feeling inspired to declutter or change your environment.
- Being invited into spaces or conversations that mirror your goals.
- Having dreams that connect you with your future self.

These aren't proof in the conventional sense. But they are alignment markers. And alignment always precedes arrival.

When It Feels Worse Before It Feels Better

Perhaps the most misunderstood part of the manifestation process is that sometimes, things appear to get worse right before they get better. Not because you're doing something wrong—but because your system is recalibrating. Your external world may begin to release everything that doesn't match your new frequency—and that release can feel like loss, confusion, or even chaos. This is the "death before rebirth" phase. The energetic shedding. The dismantling of the old foundation to make space for the new structure. It's uncomfortable. It may come with emotional purging, fatigue, doubt, or even conflict. But it's a sign of real, deep integration.

Imagine you've been manifesting abundance, and suddenly your job ends. Or you've been calling in love, and your current relationship breaks apart. This doesn't mean you're blocked. It may mean that the container you were in couldn't hold your expansion—and so it's being cleared.

The key here is to stay present without attaching to fear. The discomfort is temporary. What matters is how you interpret it. If you see it as regression, you'll spiral. If you see it as evidence of the process, you'll move through it with grace.

Questions to ground you in this phase:

- What part of me is being asked to be released or upgraded?
- What am I making this discomfort mean about me?
- Can I stay rooted in trust even when things don't look like I expected?

Remember: the breakdown is often the initiation. And if you can stay aligned internally while the external rearranges, your manifestation won't just arrive—it will arrive cleaner, stronger, and more aligned than you imagined.

Trust the Unseen Growth

Manifestation is not always a linear climb. Sometimes it's a spiral staircase—progressing upward even when it feels like you're circling the same point. Sometimes it's invisible until, suddenly, it's undeniable. And sometimes it's working most powerfully when it looks like nothing is happening at all.

The most important shift you can make is to stop relying on evidence as your source of belief. Let belief become your source of evidence. Let your inner knowing be enough. Let your micro-decisions, emotional resilience, and growing alignment speak louder than results.

You'll know it's working not because everything is perfect, but because you are changing. You are thinking differently. You are moving with more intention. You are no longer the same person who began the journey—and that shift alone ensures the outcome must change.

In the next Chapter, we'll explore when to surrender and when to push, how to recognize energetic timing, and how to follow intuitive momentum instead of forcing your way forward. But for now, know this:

If you feel different,

if you see life through a new lens,

if you're acting from alignment rather than fear—

it's working. Even if you can't see it yet.

And soon, the world will catch up.

Chapter 12: When to Let Go vs. When to Push

One of the most misunderstood aspects of manifestation is timing. Not just when things will happen, but how to respond in the space between desire and arrival. This in-between is where most people get lost. They either grip too tightly, trying to force an outcome into existence, or they let go too soon, convinced nothing is happening. Both extremes create resistance.

Learning when to let go and when to push is about more than strategy. It's about energetic discernment. It's the art of sensing what your field, nervous system, and intuitive intelligence are telling you in any given moment. It's knowing when to surrender control and when to engage your will. And it's about learning to dance with momentum rather than wrestle with it.

This Chapter is your guide to understanding that timing is not passive. It's alive. It communicates with you. And once you learn how to read its signals, you'll stop doubting your path and start flowing with precision.

The Energetics of Surrender: Letting Go with Intention

Surrender is not giving up. It's giving over—releasing the grip of control so that the deeper intelligence of life can move through you. Letting go does not mean walking away from your desire. It means detaching from the outcome long enough to allow it to arrive in its highest form.

We often hold so tightly to what we want that we suffocate it. We demand answers, timelines, and proof. We check for signs, question ourselves, and replay the plan a hundred times in our heads. But this energy is not aligned—it's contracted. And contraction creates static in the field.

The power of surrender lies in trusting that once the desire is planted and the inner work is done, the universe is already rearranging itself on your behalf. Your job is not to micromanage the process. Your job is to remain energetically open.

You know it's time to let go when:
- You've done everything in your power without forcing.
- You're mentally and emotionally exhausted from over-efforting.
- You notice your nervous system tightening every time you think about the outcome.
- You feel the impulse to push even harder, but deep down, you know it's not the time.

In these moments, letting go becomes an act of faith. It's choosing to anchor into the present, to nurture your current life, and to trust that what you've aligned with is already on its way.

Letting go is not passive. It's deeply active. It means focusing your energy on becoming more of yourself instead of obsessing over what hasn't yet appeared. It means choosing joy, creativity, and peace—not as distractions, but as the actual vibration that allows your manifestation to land.

Aligned Effort: When to Push from Power, Not Panic

There are times when pushing is not resistance—it's resonance. It's the moment when your inner energy is aligned, your body is ready, your clarity is sharp, and the path ahead is open. This is when action becomes activation. Not as a way to chase the outcome, but as a way to embody the version of you who already lives the outcome.

Pushing from power feels very different than pushing from panic. Panic pushing comes from fear: "I need to make this happen or it never will." It's anxious, grasping, and often disconnected from intuition. Power pushing, on the other hand, feels like momentum. It's driven by clarity, not urgency. It's action that feels alive, inspired, and even fun.

You know it's time to push when:

- You feel a natural surge of energy and clarity around the next step.
- Resistance has given way to readiness—you're not acting to escape discomfort, but to step into expansion.
- Opportunities start to appear, and your system feels excited, not frozen.
- The path may not be fully visible, but you sense movement is required—and you trust yourself to take it.

Aligned effort does not mean you hustle blindly. It means you listen deeply and act precisely. You don't wait for perfect conditions, but you don't ignore your own rhythm either. You push not because you're afraid time is running out, but because you know the energy is ripe.

When you're in this state, pushing becomes a joy. It doesn't drain you—it empowers you. You feel more connected to your purpose, more confident in your steps, and more trusting in your ability to navigate what unfolds.

Reading the Signals: Timing and Intuitive Momentum

The key to knowing when to let go or when to push lies in developing a relationship with your intuitive sense of timing. This is not something you can analyze or rationalize. It's something you feel. And it often speaks in sensations, symbols, and subtle emotional cues.

Start by paying attention to your body. Your nervous system is a timing device. When it feels open, relaxed, and alert, that's a green light. When it feels tense, closed, or depleted, that's a signal to pause.

Next, tune into your environment. Life speaks through patterns. Are doors opening easily, or do they keep closing no matter how hard you try? Are people and resources showing up with grace, or is everything feeling stuck and heavy? The universe responds to readiness with synchronicity. If you're constantly hitting walls, it may be time to let go—not of the vision, but of the timing.

Another powerful way to read the signals is through your inner dialogue. Notice the tone of your thoughts around the manifestation. Are you obsessing? Doubting? Pushing from fear? Or are you feeling clear, excited, and calm—even if you're still in the unknown?

When your inner landscape is aligned, action feels like flow. When it's misaligned, action feels like friction.

There are also times when the impulse to act is subtle but persistent. A quiet inner nudge. A repeating thought. A vision that keeps coming back. These are often invitations from your future self, asking you to take a step that might not make sense yet—but carries energetic weight. When you learn to follow these nudges, you collapse time. You shift from efforting to intuiting.

The practice, then, is not to make every decision perfectly. It's to become more aware of what energy is driving your choices. Let go when the energy is contracted. Push when it's alive. Pause when you're unsure. Listen, feel, adjust. That's how timing becomes intuitive rather than intellectual.

The Dance Between Will and Surrender

Manifestation is not a battle between effort and faith. It's a dance. And you are both the dancer and the music. Some days will call for stillness. Others will call for bold movement. Some moments will ask you to trust more deeply. Others will ask you to leap.

The question is never simply, "Should I let go or push?" The real question is, "What is the most aligned use of my energy right now?"

When you master this question, you become fluid. You stop forcing. You stop waiting. You move with life instead of against it. And manifestation stops being something you try to control—and starts being something you allow, shape, and embody.

The world responds to those who understand timing. Because timing is not about patience or pressure. It's about presence. It's about knowing where you are in the rhythm of becoming—and trusting that when you honor that rhythm, life will meet you exactly where you are.

In the next Chapter, we'll step into a higher-level truth: that manifestation does not begin with results, but with identity—and that trusting the invisible timeline is the final initiation into true energetic mastery. But for now, remember this: You don't need to choose between will and surrender.

You need to know when to bow—and when to rise.

And your body, your intuition, and your energy already know.

All you have to do is listen.

PART IV: LIVING THE HIDDEN MANIFESTATION LIFE

Chapter 13: Trusting the Invisible Timeline

If there's one principle that separates those who manifest with flow from those who struggle endlessly with frustration, it's this: trust in the invisible timeline. While much of the world is conditioned to believe in linear progress, visible effort, and measurable results, manifestation operates on a subtler rhythm. Its timeline isn't dictated by logic, deadlines, or the calendar. It is woven through frequency, alignment, identity, and readiness. And most of all, it is invisible—until it's not.

You may be doing everything "right." You may feel aligned, open, clear, and intentional. Yet the result you desire seems delayed, stuck in some cosmic waiting room. This is the moment where many people give up. But this is also where the most important work happens. Because learning to trust the invisible timeline means releasing your grip on when and how—and anchoring yourself more deeply in who you are becoming.

The outcome is already on its way. The question is: will you stay in the frequency long enough for it to meet you?

Why Results Come After Identity, Not Before

Most people try to prove their worth through effort, achievement, and visible progress. They believe that once the result arrives—once the money is in the bank, the relationship is official, or the business takes off—they'll finally feel safe, empowered, or whole.

But manifestation flips that script. It demands that you feel the identity of the outcome before it shows up. That you become the version of you who already has it, even when your current reality still reflects the opposite.

This is not delusion. It's vibrational congruence. The universe is not responding to your timeline. It's responding to your readiness. And readiness isn't measured by how much you want something. It's measured by how deeply your nervous system, emotions, beliefs, and actions are attuned to the version of you who already lives in that reality.

This is why trusting the timeline is inseparable from trusting yourself. Because if you haven't yet manifested the thing you desire, it's not because you've failed—it's because your current identity cannot yet hold it. And when you try to force a result from a misaligned identity, you create energetic static.

But when you shift your identity first—when you start speaking, walking, thinking, and choosing from your future self—you activate a magnetic pull. You start collapsing time not through force, but through resonance. And then, seemingly out of nowhere, things begin to land. Not because you pushed harder, but because you matched the frequency of what you asked for.

The delay, then, is not punishment. It's preparation. And every moment you spend becoming who you need to be before the result arrives is time well invested—because it ensures that what comes to you, stays with you.

The Illusion of Stagnation and the Truth of Recalibration

One of the most difficult parts of manifestation is the phase that looks like "nothing is happening." You've done the work. You've aligned your energy. You've taken the steps. And yet, externally, your life appears unchanged. This is the moment the ego panics. It tries to fix, analyze, or abandon the path. But beneath the surface, something is always moving.

This phase is not stagnation—it is recalibration. And it's essential.

Imagine you're tuning a musical instrument. Between one note and the next, there is a pause—a subtle moment where the vibration adjusts. That moment may be silent, but it is full of movement. The same is true in your life. When you've shifted internally, your external world needs time to catch up. The old reality begins to dissolve, but the new one hasn't fully materialized yet. That space in-between is sacred. It's the cocoon between the caterpillar and the butterfly.

In this space, your job is not to rush forward—it's to stabilize. To hold your frequency. To walk with integrity. To breathe through the discomfort of uncertainty without collapsing into doubt.

This is where many people lose the thread. They confuse silence with failure. They assume absence of results means misalignment. But manifestation is not linear—it's dimensional. It involves energies, people, situations, and timing aligning in ways you cannot see. What looks like a delay is often the precise orchestration of multiple threads coming into place.

During recalibration, you might feel like:

- Old habits or people are falling away faster than new ones are arriving.

- You feel emotionally raw, even though nothing "bad" is happening.

- You experience random setbacks that test your clarity and patience.

- You alternate between peace and frustration without warning.

These are not signs of regression. They are signs of a system reordering itself around a new vibration. And your only real task is to not interrupt the process. Hold your energy like it's sacred. Move with intention. Nourish your nervous system. Trust that life is moving—even when it moves invisibly. And remember: every day you embody your new identity, you speed up the manifestation—not by chasing it, but by magnetizing it.

Becoming a Steward of Timing Instead of a Slave to It

When you release the need to control timing, you become infinitely more powerful. You stop being reactive and start becoming responsive. You don't panic when something takes longer than expected. You don't shrink when someone else "gets there first." You no longer measure your progress against external timelines, but by internal coherence.

This shift allows you to become a steward of timing—someone who knows how to work with life instead of against it. You recognize that just as nature has seasons, so do your manifestations. And every season is necessary.

There is the **planting season**—where you set intentions, align your energy, and envision your future. There is the **growth season**—where you do the inner and outer work, regulate your nervous system, and upgrade your identity. There is the **integration season**—where everything seems still but is actually recalibrating. And then there is the **harvest season**—where the results arrive often all at once, seemingly out of nowhere.

Trying to force a harvest in the planting season is not ambitious—it's premature. And trying to abandon the process in the integration season is not protective—it's self-sabotage.

To become a steward of timing is to live in rhythm. It's to know that what is yours is already encoded in your field—and the more you stabilize your signal, the faster it finds you. It's to stop rushing through life and start relating to life as a co-creator, not a taskmaster.

Practical ways to embody this stewardship include:

- Daily rituals that anchor your identity, even when results are not visible.
- Journaling evidence of inner shifts, synchronicities, and subtle wins.
- Celebrating progress you feel, not just what you can measure.

- Redirecting anxious energy into creation, play, or rest.
- Asking: Who am I becoming right now, and how can I honor that becoming?

When you live like this, time stops being your enemy. It becomes your partner. And the invisible timeline becomes something you trust—not because you see it, but because you know it.

The Timeline Is Already Running

You are not waiting for your manifestation to begin. It has already begun. The moment you set the desire with clarity, aligned your energy, and took even one step forward, the timeline activated. What you desire is not "out there"—it is in process. In progress. In motion.

Your work is not to measure the distance between where you are and where you want to be. Your work is to become a match for the moment when the result arrives. Because it will arrive—not because you forced it, but because you stayed long enough in the energy of receiving.

This is what it means to trust the invisible timeline. To live in devotion to who you are becoming. To believe in unseen forces. To honor your own rhythm. And to recognize that manifestation is not a reward—it's a reflection.

In the next Chapter, we'll explore the protective power of magnetic boundaries—how to keep your field clean, clear, and aligned so your manifestations land in integrity and with ease. But for now, hold this truth close: The timeline is not broken.

It's unfolding.

And your only task is to keep becoming the one who's ready.

Chapter 14: Magnetic Boundaries = Magnetic Manifestation

Manifestation is not just about what you attract—it's also about what you allow. And one of the most powerful yet overlooked aspects of allowing is the strength and clarity of your boundaries. Energetically, you are always in relationship: with people, environments, ideas, habits, and your own inner world. Every one of these relationships affects your frequency. And if your boundaries are weak, blurred, or reactive, your energy leaks—distorting the very signal you're sending out into the universe.

Magnetic manifestation requires a clean field. And a clean field requires clear boundaries. Boundaries are not walls you put up to push people away. They are energetic filters that protect what you're creating, uphold your values, and reflect your worth. They signal to the universe: "I take my energy seriously. I respect my vision. I only allow what matches the reality I'm building."

In this Chapter, we'll explore how magnetic boundaries make your manifestation field more potent, why setting them is an act of self-trust, and how to protect your energy without withdrawing from the world.

Boundaries as a Frequency Filter

Every interaction you have—every conversation, commitment, and agreement—is a transmission of energy. When you say yes to things that drain you, tolerate dynamics that misalign with your values, or absorb the emotions of others without discernment, you weaken your frequency. You're not just tired—you're out of resonance.

This happens subtly. You might justify it as being "nice," "available," or "open." But beneath the surface, your field is picking up static. And that static sends mixed signals. You may be asking the universe for expansion while energetically agreeing to constriction. You may be affirming your worth in your journal while living in relationships that undermine it. These contradictions dilute your manifestation power.

Boundaries are how you create coherence. They say: "This is what I'm available for. This is what I won't carry. This is where I begin and you end." And that clarity sharpens your frequency. You become easier to read—not just by people, but by reality itself. Your yes becomes clean. Your no becomes non-negotiable. And your manifestations arrive faster, because there's less distortion in the field.

Ask yourself:

- Where in my life do I feel emotionally or energetically foggy?
- What am I tolerating that I've outgrown?
- Who or what consistently pulls me out of alignment—and why am I still allowing it?

These questions are not about blame. They're about calibration. Because every time you uphold a boundary, you reinforce the reality you're building. You tell your nervous system: "This is safe. This is real. This is who I am now." And from that clarity, life responds.

Saying No as an Energetic Yes

One of the most powerful shifts in boundary work is realizing that every no you give is also a yes—to something greater. When you say no to chaos, you say yes to clarity. When you say no to self-abandonment, you say yes to self-respect. When you say no to misaligned energy, you create space for what's meant for you to arrive.

Too often, we fear that setting boundaries will push things away. But in truth, boundaries do the opposite: they magnetize. They purify your field so that only what is truly meant for your next level can enter. Without them, you're constantly managing the weight of what no longer fits—leaving no room for what could.

Many people struggle to say no because they've been taught that boundaries are selfish or harsh. They worry about disappointing others, losing love, or being misunderstood. But manifestation is not about being agreeable—it's about being authentic. And authenticity often requires discernment, even when it's uncomfortable.

To begin reclaiming your energetic space, start practicing small no's. The ones that don't feel threatening, but still build your muscle of truth. Decline a social invitation that drains you. Unfollow accounts that trigger comparison. Say no to a project that doesn't light you up. These are not trivial choices—they are energetic declarations. And each one strengthens the field around you.

Eventually, your no becomes an extension of your power. Not a barrier, but a beacon. It lets others know where you stand. It lets the universe know what you're ready for. And it lets you feel the integrity of living in alignment with your future self.

Protecting the Field Without Hiding from Life

Creating strong boundaries doesn't mean isolating yourself or living in fear of being drained. In fact, the most magnetic people are often the most open—because they know how to protect their energy. They move through the world with presence, but not absorption. They connect deeply, but don't fuse. They give generously, but not at the cost of depletion.

True boundaries are not about withdrawal. They're about clarity. When you trust yourself to set and uphold boundaries, you no longer need to be hyper-vigilant. You stop scanning for threats. You stop filtering your intuition through anxiety. Instead, you relax into a deeper sense of inner safety—and that relaxation makes you more receptive.

Think of it this way: if your energetic field were a home, boundaries would be the walls, the doors, the locks, and the invitation list. You wouldn't leave your front door open all day for strangers to walk through—and yet many people do exactly that with their energy. They absorb every emotion, respond to every request, and say yes before checking in with themselves.

To protect your field, start by cultivating energetic hygiene:

- Begin each day with a grounding practice—visualization, breathwork, or simply placing your hand on your heart and stating your intention.
- Notice where your energy leaks throughout the day. Is it in conversations? Social media? Overcommitting? Make note of where you feel a contraction.
- Before saying yes to anything, ask: Is this aligned with the version of me I'm becoming? If the answer isn't clear, give yourself time.

You can also visualize your field as a protective aura—strong, luminous, and responsive. Let it filter what enters. Let it bounce off what's not for you. Not through force, but through sovereignty.

Remember: boundaries are not something you impose on others. They are something you maintain within yourself. Others will feel your clarity and either rise to meet it—or fall away. Both outcomes are sacred.

Boundaries Are a Manifestation Tool

Boundaries are not a detour from the manifestation path. They are the path. Because without them, your energy is scattered. Your field is muddied. Your desires are contradicted. And your results are inconsistent.

When you live with magnetic boundaries, you don't just protect your energy—you amplify it. You send a signal to the universe that says: I know what I want. I know what I deserve. And I'm willing to say no to everything that isn't that.

This isn't about being rigid or unkind. It's about being honest. It's about respecting your vision enough to curate your environment. And it's about becoming the kind of person who can hold what they've asked for—not just attract it, but sustain it.

In the next Chapter, we'll move even deeper into this frequency of wholeness—exploring how to manifest not from craving, but from fullness. Because the most powerful manifestation doesn't come from wanting more. It comes from being more.

But first, ask yourself: where does my energy go when I'm not paying attention? What am I allowing that no longer aligns? And what might become possible if I protected my field like it mattered?

Because it does.

And the universe is watching.

Chapter 15: Beyond Desire: Manifesting from Wholeness

Most people begin their manifestation journey from a place of longing. They want more—more money, more love, more health, more freedom—and they believe that having more will make them feel better. This desire is natural, and in many ways, it is the spark that initiates transformation. But desire is only the beginning of the path, not the destination.

True, sustainable manifestation doesn't come from craving or striving. It comes from wholeness. From realizing that you are already complete, already worthy, already enough. When you manifest from wholeness, your desires are no longer a substitute for your identity or emotional safety. They become extensions of your fullness, expressions of your evolution—not requirements for your self-worth.

This Chapter is an invitation to evolve your manifestation practice from want-based to wholeness-based. To move beyond chasing outcomes and step into the frequency of already-being. Because when you manifest from wholeness, you are not reaching for something outside yourself—you are aligning with what's already true on the deepest level.

Wholeness Is Not the Absence of Desire

To manifest from wholeness does not mean you no longer want anything. It means you are no longer dependent on the outcome to validate your sense of self. You still have goals, intentions, and preferences—but they arise from creativity, not lack.

This distinction is critical. Many people confuse spiritual growth with detachment that becomes apathy. They try to suppress their desires in an effort to be "enlightened" or "non-attached." But true wholeness is not emptiness. It is fullness. It is the realization that you can desire something and know that you are whole without it.

When your desires emerge from wholeness, they feel different. There's no panic. No pressure. No sense of "If this doesn't happen, I'm not okay." Instead, your energy is soft, open, trusting. You move toward the vision because it excites you, not because you believe your life depends on it.

Desire from lack says, "I'll be whole when this shows up."

Desire from wholeness says, "I'm whole, and this would be beautiful to experience."

This energetic difference is everything. Because the universe responds not to your words, but to your vibration. And when you radiate the energy of completeness, you become magnetic. Not because you're trying to pull things in—but because you are no longer repelling them with fear, need, or insecurity. So the work is not to eliminate desire. It's to clean it. To purify it of desperation and replace it with devotion. To ask: "Why do I want this?" and "Who am I without it?" and "Can I love myself here, even before it arrives?"

When you can answer yes, you're manifesting from wholeness.

The Trap of Chasing Completion Through Creation

One of the most seductive illusions in manifestation is the belief that success, wealth, or love will complete you. That when you reach a certain level, achieve the vision, or finally receive what you've been working for, then you will feel whole.

But manifestation rooted in incompleteness often leads to burnout, disillusionment, or shallow victories. You might reach the goal—but find that it doesn't give you what you thought it would. The high is short-lived. The emptiness returns. And so you set a new goal, hoping this time it will fill the void.

This is the trap of chasing completion through creation. And it's exhausting.

True creation comes from overflow, not emptiness. When you create from wholeness, your vision becomes an offering. Your work becomes an act of expression, not compensation. You stop trying to earn your worth and start embodying it. You no longer need your success to prove anything. You simply let it flow from who you already are.

This doesn't mean you stop evolving. It means you stop escaping. You face the parts of yourself that feel unlovable or broken—not with shame, but with compassion. You heal the wounds that tell you you're not enough. You stop making your worth conditional on outcomes. And in doing so, you liberate your energy.

You stop manifesting from pain, and you start manifesting from peace.

Ask yourself:

- What am I hoping this manifestation will fix?
- What part of me feels like it's not enough without this?
- Can I tend to that part now, so the desire no longer has to carry that weight?

This inner work doesn't slow down manifestation. It accelerates it. Because when you are no longer attached to the outcome saving you, you become more aligned with the version of you who simply receives.

Becoming the Source Instead of the Seeker

When you manifest from wholeness, you stop outsourcing power. You no longer see reality as something to beg from, but as something to partner with. You stop seeing the universe as a vending machine and start relating to it as a mirror. What you receive reflects what you already hold inside.

This is the moment you stop being the seeker—and start being the source.

Most people are taught to believe that joy, love, and abundance exist outside of them. They're told to search for it in money, relationships, titles, and achievements. But this search often leaves them feeling hollow. Because what they're really looking for is not out there—it's within.

Becoming the source means realizing that everything you seek already exists in you as a potential frequency. That you can generate the feeling of success before the success arrives. That you can experience the vibration of love before anyone else gives it to you. That you can embody peace, power, or prosperity now—not someday.

This is not spiritual theory. It's energetic fact. When you learn to generate from within, your outer world has no choice but to match it. You stop reacting to circumstances and start creating from your center. You stop chasing and start magnetizing.

Becoming the source means:

- Practicing the emotions you wish to feel more often, regardless of circumstances.
- Creating beauty, meaning, and value from your current state—not your future one.
- Building a relationship with your inner self that is more nurturing than any external validation could ever be.

And from that place, life becomes a reflection, not a transaction. Your manifestations don't arrive to complete you. They arrive to echo your wholeness.

Want Less, Become More

The deepest manifestation is not about getting more. It's about becoming more. More aligned. More rooted. More expressed. More true.

When you want less—not because you're detached, but because you're full—you clear the space for life to bring you exactly what matches your authentic essence.

Not the performance. Not the proving. But the real you.

Desire becomes less about fixing and more about creating. You stop waiting for your life to begin and realize it's already happening now. You stop putting your power in the hands of outcomes and reclaim it as something you carry within. You are not manifesting because you are incomplete. You are manifesting because you are overflowing with vision, purpose, and presence. And when you remember that, you stop reaching. You start radiating.

In the next Chapter, we'll explore what it truly means to be the source of your own reality—not dependent on tools, techniques, or external guidance, but sovereign and self-sourced. Because wholeness is not a destination. It is your starting point. And everything you've ever wanted has been waiting for you there.

Chapter 16: Self-Sourcing Your Reality

For most of your life, you've likely been taught to look outside yourself for answers—for structure, validation, guidance, and power. You were told to follow experts, lean on systems, chase credentials, and wait for permission. Even within the spiritual or manifestation space, the same pattern persists. People turn to gurus, tools, rituals, or external signs to feel safe, to feel aligned, or to feel worthy of receiving.

But the truth is: all of these tools are secondary. They can be supportive, yes—but they are not the source. You are. Self-sourcing your reality means no longer outsourcing your power to techniques, timelines, or people. It means remembering that everything you're trying to access "out there" is actually already within you—available through your own intuition, alignment, presence, and embodied wisdom.

This Chapter is an invitation to come home to your inner authority. To release the crutches, distractions, and dependency loops that dilute your frequency. And to realize that the most powerful, sustainable manifestation happens when you stop chasing what you already are—and start sourcing it directly from your own being.

From Tool Dependency to Inner Mastery

There's nothing inherently wrong with manifestation tools. Vision boards, affirmations, crystals, full moon rituals, scripting, journaling—they can all be useful entry points. They help focus the mind, regulate the nervous system, and anchor intentions in physical form. But they are only powerful when used from a place of clarity and self-connection.

The problem arises when the tool becomes a replacement for inner knowing. When you begin to believe that if you miss a ritual, or don't follow a certain process, your manifestation won't work. This belief, while subtle, is a form of disempowerment. It places your creative authority outside of yourself, making you dependent on something external to "activate" your power.

This kind of tool dependency leads to anxiety, superstition, and performance. You begin to use the tools from fear rather than faith. You search for the "right" method instead of listening to your intuition. You micromanage every step instead of allowing the universe to co-create with your energy.

Self-sourcing flips this dynamic entirely. It doesn't reject tools—it just puts them in their rightful place. It reminds you that you are the signal, not the symbol. The power doesn't live in the journal. It lives in the you who is aligned when you write in it. The magic isn't in the ritual. It's in the you who is present when performing it.

When you stop needing tools and start choosing them, you reclaim sovereignty. You become the one who decides what works—not because someone said so, but because you feel it in your body. You move from blind following to intentional creation. And your manifestations become cleaner, faster, and more stable—because they're being sourced from the deepest part of you.

The Shift from Seeking to Sensing

One of the most liberating shifts in self-sourcing is learning to move from seeking external signs to sensing internal signals. In the early stages of manifestation, it's normal to look for signs from the universe. Angel numbers, synchronicities, messages, repeating patterns—they all feel like guidance, and they often are.

But as you evolve, you realize that the most reliable guidance comes not from something you see "out there," but from what you feel in your inner field. Your body is a tuning fork. Your intuition is a compass. Your emotional system is a feedback mechanism. When you are self-sourced, you stop needing constant reassurance from the outside world because you can sense when something is aligned or not.

This means:

- You trust the felt sense of resonance, even when logic disagrees.
- You notice energetic contraction as a signal to pause—not as a reason to panic.
- You let your inner "yes" and "no" guide your decisions, even when they defy expectation.
- You stop needing a reason to trust yourself—and start doing it because it's who you are.

Moving from seeking to sensing requires practice. It requires slowing down enough to hear yourself. It requires turning down the noise of the world so you can tune into your own frequency. But over time, this becomes your new normal. You stop second-guessing. You stop waiting for permission. You move when it feels right—not when someone tells you to.

And in that space, you become magnetic. Because nothing is more attractive than someone who trusts their own timing, their own voice, and their own vision.

Creating from Wholeness, Holding with Power

When you are self-sourced, your creations are no longer rooted in performance or proving. You're not trying to manifest to gain approval, escape a wound, or "catch up" with others. You're creating because it's your nature. Because your energy is overflowing. Because your life is a reflection of your own inner relationship—and you choose to express it through the external.

From this space, you don't chase results. You invite them. You don't cling to outcomes. You hold space for them. You don't lose yourself when things take time. You deepen into your own foundation.

This is where true manifestation lives—not in desperate action, but in embodied presence.

To sustain this level of self-sourcing, you must practice holding power. Power is not dominance. It's not perfection. It's the ability to remain centered in yourself, regardless of external fluctuations. It's the ability to hold your vision without begging. To hold your energy without leaking. To hold your standards without apology.

It means:

- Continuing to walk in your truth, even when others don't understand it.
- Continuing to honor your boundaries, even when it's inconvenient.
- Continuing to invest in your alignment, even when results haven't shown up yet.

This level of consistency creates trust—within yourself and with the universe. Because the universe doesn't just respond to what you say you want. It responds to the version of you who keeps showing up in alignment, whether or not there's applause, evidence, or validation.

You become someone who can be trusted with more—because you're no longer creating from survival, but from sovereignty.

You Were Always the Source

The most powerful truth of manifestation is also the simplest: you are the source. Not because you've mastered every technique. Not because you've read every book. But because your being—your presence, your clarity, your intention—is enough. It always was.

When you stop looking outside yourself for validation, activation, or confirmation, you reclaim the core of your power. You no longer ride the rollercoaster of external outcomes. You no longer wait for signs to feel certain. You know who you are. You know what you're here to create. And you know that it begins with you.

This is the final liberation: becoming the generator of your own energy, the guide of your own path, and the source of your own reality.

In the next Chapter, we'll explore what it looks like when this embodiment truly takes hold—how to recognize when you've shifted into a new frequency, how to live from that space, and how to trust the new version of you that's now leading the way.

But for now, remember this:

You are not here to follow.

 You are here to lead—yourself.

 And the most powerful manifestation begins the moment you stop seeking outside,

 and start sourcing from within.

PART V: FROM HIDDEN TO MASTERFUL

Chapter 17: The 7 Signs You've Shifted Frequencies

One of the most important questions in any manifestation journey is this: how do I know I've actually changed? When you've been doing deep inner work—clearing old patterns, upgrading your identity, regulating your nervous system, shifting your emotional baseline—it's natural to want confirmation. Not just external proof in the form of results, but internal markers that show you're not the same person you were when you started.

The thing is, frequency shifts are often subtle. They happen inside first. And because they don't always come with fireworks, you might overlook them. But there are unmistakable signs—patterns in your behavior, perception, and energy—that reveal when you've truly upgraded your state of being. These are not temporary highs. They are indicators of stabilization. And once you stabilize a higher frequency, manifestation becomes inevitable. Because now, your internal world matches the external reality you've been asking for.

In this Chapter, we'll explore seven key signs that show you've shifted frequencies—and why recognizing them is more powerful than waiting for results.

1. You React Differently to the Same Triggers

One of the most obvious signs that your frequency has changed is that your reactions have changed. The same people, situations, or challenges that once triggered you no longer hold the same emotional charge. You might still notice the discomfort, but you don't spiral into it. You observe it, acknowledge it, and respond with more spaciousness.

This doesn't mean you've become numb or disconnected. It means you've upgraded your nervous system's default response. You're no longer operating from survival mode. You don't need to prove, defend, or collapse. You have

access to more choices, more curiosity, more power in the pause.
This shift is especially clear when you find yourself in familiar scenarios—like family gatherings, work dynamics, or intimate relationships—and realize you're not triggered the way you used to be. You might even feel neutral, compassionate, or amused, where you once felt attacked or overwhelmed.
This is not a small win. This is energetic mastery. Because how you respond determines the **reality you create next. And when your reactions change, your timeline changes with them.**

2. You No Longer Chase the Old Timeline

Another strong indicator that you've shifted frequencies is that you no longer feel attached to outdated dreams, identities, or relationships. What once felt urgent or desirable now feels complete—or even irrelevant. You're not abandoning your vision; you're simply refining it. Your preferences are evolving to match your new energetic state.

This can be disorienting. You might look at old goals and think, Why did I want that so badly? You might feel confused about your direction, not because you're lost, but because you're no longer clinging to what was. Your energy is updating faster than your mind can keep up—and that's a good thing.

Letting go of the old timeline is not a failure. It's evidence of growth. It shows you're no longer trying to manifest from an outdated self-concept. Instead, you're allowing space for a future that reflects who you are now, not who you used to be.

You might feel:

- A sudden disinterest in proving yourself.
- A loss of urgency to "arrive" anywhere.
- A quiet satisfaction in the present moment, even as the next vision

builds.
- A deeper trust in your timing and path.

This shift marks a turning point. You're no longer chasing life. You're aligning with it.

3. Your Inner Dialogue Is Kinder, Clearer, and More Grounded

A massive frequency upgrade shows up in how you speak to yourself. If you've been doing inner work, you'll start to notice that your self-talk becomes less punitive and more encouraging. You don't shame yourself for mistakes. You don't spiral into self-criticism. You start relating to yourself with compassion. This change doesn't require effort—it emerges organically. You simply notice that your thoughts sound different. They feel like they're coming from a wiser, calmer version of you. You trust yourself more. You stop gaslighting your own intuition. You give yourself the benefit of the doubt.

And when fear arises, you don't make it mean something's wrong. You hold it, move with it, and stay anchored in truth.

This shift in inner dialogue is not about perfection. It's about pattern recognition. You've practiced alignment long enough that your inner voice has recalibrated. And that new voice creates new outcomes—because manifestation is language-dependent. The words you think, speak, and feel shape your field. When your internal language shifts, reality responds.

4. You Prioritize Alignment Over Outcome

One of the most mature signs of frequency elevation is this: you care more about staying in alignment than getting the thing.

You might still want the manifestation. But you no longer sacrifice your peace, boundaries, or truth to force it into being. You trust that if something costs you your energy, it's not aligned. You trust that the right thing will not require you to abandon yourself.

This shift is subtle but massive. It's the end of desperation. It's the beginning of sovereignty. You become less fixated on "how" and more devoted to how you feel in the process.

You know your job is to hold the frequency—not to manipulate the outcome. That means:

- Saying no to opportunities that don't resonate, even if they look good on paper.
- Walking away from relationships that don't reflect your worth.
- Resting instead of pushing through misaligned effort.
- Trusting that your energy is more valuable than your productivity.

You realize: alignment is the outcome. And once that clicks, manifestation becomes a byproduct, not a project.

5. You Experience "Clean Wins" That Require Less Effort

As your frequency stabilizes, you start to experience manifestations that arrive with ease, speed, and little resistance. These are "clean wins"—opportunities, connections, or results that come without hustle, drama, or compromise.

They show up as:

- An unexpected offer that aligns perfectly.
- A chance encounter that opens a new door.
- A solution arriving exactly when you stopped overthinking.

What makes these wins different isn't just the outcome—it's the feeling. There's no inner chaos. No attachment. Just a calm sense of, Of course this happened. These moments are signs that your field is matching your vision. You're no longer creating from effort, but from energetic clarity. You're letting life meet you, not chase you.

And the more you experience these wins, the more you trust the process—not because it's perfect, but because you are finally attuned to your own power.

6. You Attract People Who Reflect Your New Identity

Frequency shifts change who you attract. As you elevate, your relationships upgrade. You start meeting people who reflect your values, mirror your growth, and challenge you in expansive ways—not draining ones.

This shift might mean:

- Old friends or dynamics fall away without conflict.
- You feel drawn to new communities, mentors, or collaborations.
- Conversations become more aligned, nourishing, and purpose-driven.
- You feel more seen, supported, and inspired by your connections.

This is not a coincidence. It's resonance. You've shifted internally, and your outer world is realigning. Relationships are one of the fastest ways to read your frequency. Who you allow in your space—and how they treat you—is a reflection of what you believe you're worthy of.

When your relationships evolve, it's not about superiority. It's about integrity. You're simply no longer available for energies that don't match your vision.

7. You Feel Peace Even Without the Proof

Perhaps the deepest sign that you've shifted frequencies is that you feel a strange, surprising peace—even when the manifestation hasn't arrived. You no longer need proof to feel confident. You are the proof.

This peace is not complacency. It's not giving up. It's an embodied knowing that what's meant for you is already in motion. You feel anchored. You feel whole. You feel ready—not just for the thing, but for the version of you who lives in that reality.

You no longer fear the unknown. You make decisions without panic. You move from presence. And you trust yourself to handle what comes.

This is the frequency that bends reality. This is what makes the invisible become visible.

You've Already Shifted—Now Stabilize It

Frequency shifts aren't always loud. They don't always come with instant evidence. But when you start recognizing these internal signs, you stop doubting. You realize: I've already changed. Now it's just about staying in the new state long enough for the external to catch up.

Don't rush back to the old frequency because you don't see results yet. Don't sabotage your evolution by looking for validation outside of yourself. If you feel more peaceful, more trusting, more aligned, more you—you've already shifted. Now the work is simple: stay there. Deepen it. Let it become your new normal. And watch as the world rearranges around the person you've become.

In the next Chapter, we'll uncover the most common mistakes that sabotage manifestation and how to move through them with clarity—so that you don't undo what you've worked so hard to shift. For now, hold this truth:

You don't need confirmation.

You are the confirmation.

And your life is already listening.

Chapter 18: Common Mistakes That Kill Manifestations

As powerful as manifestation can be, it's equally easy to sabotage. Often, the reasons your desires aren't materializing have nothing to do with effort, intention, or the universe ignoring you—and everything to do with subtle, often unconscious habits that distort your frequency, block your receptivity, or keep you cycling in outdated energy.

These mistakes aren't flaws in character. They're simply patterns—learned ways of being that made sense in the past but no longer support your evolution. The good news is that once you become aware of them, you can shift them. Awareness is the first step in realignment. And the more honest you are about what might be interrupting your flow, the more quickly you can get back on track.

This Chapter is a deep dive into the most common traps that kill manifestation energy: fear-based creation, forcing outcomes, and over-efforting from misaligned motivation. As you read, reflect gently. You don't need to judge yourself—you just need to see clearly. Because clarity is power. And sometimes, the smallest shift in approach can open the biggest portal to receiving.

Fear-Based Creation: Manifesting from the Wound, Not the Soul

Many people begin their manifestation journey from a place of pain. They want to escape scarcity, avoid rejection, or fix a feeling of unworthiness. And while that's understandable—it's also unsustainable. When your desire is fueled primarily by fear, your frequency carries that fear into everything you create. You might attract temporary results. You might even see quick wins. But they don't last, because the foundation is shaky. Your nervous system doesn't feel safe receiving or sustaining the manifestation. And so, without realizing it, you create circumstances that reflect the very fear you were trying to outrun.

Fear-based creation often looks like:

- Wanting money because you're terrified of lack.
- Seeking love to avoid loneliness.
- Pursuing success to prove your worth.

There's nothing wrong with wanting these things. But when the motivation is fear, the energy becomes distorted. You are sending a signal to the universe that says, "I need this or I'm not okay." And that energy creates tension, urgency, and misalignment.

The shift comes when you begin to feel safe within yourself—before the result arrives. When you affirm your own worth, your own enoughness, your own capacity to hold joy, connection, and abundance. Then, your desires are no longer band-aids. They become celebrations of your growth.

To shift out of fear-based creation, ask:

- Is my desire coming from inspiration or desperation?
- If this never happened, would I still know I'm enough?
- What would it feel like to want this from a place of wholeness?

When you ask these questions honestly, you begin to manifest from soul—not from the wound.

Forcing the Outcome: Controlling Instead of Co-Creating

Another mistake that blocks manifestation is the urge to control. You set an intention, and instead of allowing space for the universe to co-create with you, you try to manage every step. You obsess over timelines. You micromanage details. You demand signs, proof, and progress on your schedule.

This habit is rooted in fear and mistrust. You don't believe that what you desire is unfolding unless you can see it happening. And so, rather than remaining in energetic alignment, you grip tighter. You check constantly. You overthink every decision.

This control creates resistance. It clogs your field with anxiety. It pulls your focus away from the state of being you're cultivating and back into external measurement. And paradoxically, the more you force, the further the result drifts from you.

The truth is: manifestation is not a vending machine. You don't input a desire and get a result on demand. It's a dance—a collaboration between your inner world and the outer universe. And that dance requires trust.

Here's what trusting looks like:
- Taking aligned action when called, not just for the sake of movement.
- Releasing the need to know exactly how or when.
- Staying anchored in your vibration even when reality hasn't caught up.
- Focusing more on becoming than on managing.

To shift out of force, ask:
- Where am I gripping instead of allowing?
- What might happen if I released control and returned to alignment?
- Do I trust myself to handle the unfolding?

Manifestation requires momentum—but it also requires surrender. If you're pushing too hard, you're probably trying to do the universe's job. And that job was never yours to begin with.

Over-Efforting from Misaligned Motivation

Perhaps the most exhausting mistake on the manifestation path is trying to earn what you already deserve. Many people have internalized the belief that effort equals worth. That if they work hard enough, sacrifice enough, or prove themselves relentlessly, they'll finally be rewarded.

This often shows up as:
- Hustling endlessly toward goals that don't feel good.
- Over-delivering in relationships to be chosen.
- Performing productivity to mask inner doubt.
- Burnout disguised as ambition.

The problem isn't the effort—it's the energy behind it. If your actions are driven by guilt, shame, or self-doubt, they send a signal of lack. You are broadcasting the frequency of "I'm not enough yet." And that frequency delays or distorts your manifestations.

When you shift into aligned effort, everything changes. You still show up. You still move forward. But your actions are sourced from joy, clarity, and self-trust—not fear. You rest when needed. You act with precision. You don't confuse busyness with progress.

Aligned effort feels like:

- A deep yes in your body, even if there's challenge.
- Creative flow instead of constant fatigue.
- Clear boundaries around your energy.
- A sense of expansion instead of contraction.

To course-correct, ask:

- Am I acting from alignment or proving?
- What would it look like to trust that I am already worthy?
- Can I allow more ease, not because I'm lazy—but because I'm in resonance?

The truth is, the universe does not reward exhaustion. It rewards integrity. When your effort aligns with your authentic energy, results arrive with less strain and more grace.

Mistakes Are Just Messages

If you've made these mistakes—welcome. Every creator has. They're not failures. They're invitations. Each one reveals where your frequency is still being shaped, healed, and refined. They point you back toward your power.

Manifestation isn't about being perfect. It's about being present. Present enough to notice when you're acting from fear instead of truth. Present enough to feel when effort becomes resistance. Present enough to shift—without shame—back into alignment.

So let go of the pressure to get it all right. Let go of the illusion that you can force your way into a new reality. Let go of the story that says you must do more to be more.

Instead, return. Return to the version of you who knows. Return to the version of you who trusts. Return to the version of you who creates not to escape—but to express.

In the next Chapter, we'll move beyond these patterns entirely. We'll explore what it means to make manifestation not just a practice, but a lifestyle—a natural, integrated way of being. Because once you stop chasing and start living from alignment, you'll see that the greatest manifestation is who you've become.

Chapter 19: Creating Reality as a Lifestyle, Not a Hack

There comes a point in the manifestation journey where you realize this isn't something you do—it's something you are. It's no longer about scripting at full moons or repeating affirmations ten times a day. It's no longer about trying to attract a specific outcome with just the right technique. It's about the way you live—how you think, feel, act, and respond every single day. Manifestation stops being a hack or shortcut and starts becoming a way of moving through the world.

When you reach this level, you're no longer chasing results. You're embodying the frequency of the life you've chosen to align with. You trust the unseen, even when the seen hasn't arrived. You don't fall apart when things take time. You don't oscillate between action and doubt. You stabilize. You hold. You become. This Chapter is about that lifestyle. It's about what it looks like to live as someone who knows they are the source. It's about shifting from technique-based manifestation into identity-based embodiment, where your frequency is your compass, your choices are your signal, and your life becomes a direct mirror of your inner reality.

Manifestation as Expression, Not Escape

One of the clearest signs that you're living manifestation as a lifestyle is that your desires come from a space of expression, not escape. In the early stages of growth, it's common to want things because you're trying to avoid something: the job you hate, the loneliness you feel, the financial stress that's wearing you down. That's normal—but it's reactive. It's survival-mode dreaming.

When manifestation becomes your lifestyle, your desires are no longer rooted in fixing or fleeing. They're rooted in expanding. You want things because they're aligned with your evolution—not because they're a remedy for pain. You're not trying to escape your life. You're trying to amplify it.

This means your goals start to feel different. You're not building a business just to quit your job—you're building because it excites your soul. You're not calling in love because you're afraid to be alone—you're calling it in because you have so much to share. You're not asking for more money because you're afraid of not having enough—you're asking because you're ready to steward more impact.

This shift changes everything. You're no longer moving from urgency. You're moving from purpose. And when you move from purpose, life meets you differently. You become less interested in chasing highs or proving worth and more devoted to sustaining peace, power, and expansion.

To live like this means you start curating your reality every day—not just when you want something. You refine your environment, your relationships, your habits, and your language to match who you are becoming. You live from your future self, not your past self. And every part of your life becomes an act of alignment.

Consistent Identity Equals Consistent Reality

Manifestation becomes a lifestyle when identity stops fluctuating. When you stop being the person who wants it on Monday, doubts it on Tuesday, overworks for it on Wednesday, and gives up by Friday. That inconsistency sends mixed signals. It collapses your field. And it makes manifestation feel like guesswork.

But when your identity stabilizes—when you consistently think, speak, and act as the version of you who already has the thing—then the manifestation doesn't need to be forced. It becomes inevitable.

This version of you:

- Makes choices from your desired reality, not your current one.
- Aligns daily habits with long-term energy, not short-term moods.

- Embodies the values of your future self, even when results haven't arrived yet.

For example, if you're manifesting financial freedom, the lifestyle version of that is not just visualizing wealth. It's making financial decisions from abundance—not lack. It's releasing shame around money. It's setting boundaries with your time. It's walking with the self-respect of someone who owns their worth, regardless of current income.

If you're manifesting love, the lifestyle version isn't obsessing over dating apps. It's cultivating self-love, emotional intelligence, and clear communication—so that when love arrives, you can hold it.

If you're manifesting purpose, the lifestyle version is not endlessly searching for it. It's showing up today in ways that feel meaningful, generous, and alive.

The point is, manifestation doesn't begin with the result. It begins with you. And the more consistent your identity becomes, the faster reality follows.

Ask yourself:

- What would my future self not tolerate anymore?
- How does my future self begin their day?
- What choices feel most congruent with my next-level life?

These aren't lofty concepts. They're everyday decisions. And when made consistently, they build a reality that no longer requires "manifesting tricks"—because your life is the manifestation.

Daily Alignment Habits that Sustain Your Frequency

To make manifestation a lifestyle, you need more than big breakthroughs—you need daily alignment. You need rituals, practices, and systems that hold you steady when things feel uncertain. You need a foundation that doesn't collapse under the weight of waiting.

These aren't meant to be rigid routines. They're meant to be recalibration tools—things that help you return to your chosen frequency again and again, no matter what's happening around you.

Here are some powerful alignment habits that anchor the manifestation lifestyle:

1. Morning Intentionality

Start the day as the version of you who's already aligned. Even ten minutes of breathwork, journaling, or setting a clear intention can shift your entire frequency. Don't check your phone first thing. Check in with your energy.

2. Energetic Check-Ins Throughout the Day

Pause and ask, "Am I acting from the version of me I'm becoming—or the version I've outgrown?" These check-ins help you make small but powerful course corrections that keep you on the aligned path.

3. Emotional Regulation Practices

Your emotions are not problems—they're indicators. When you feel out of alignment, don't suppress it. Breathe into it. Move your body. Use EFT tapping, somatic techniques, or even a walk to reset your nervous system.

4. Visualization with Feeling, Not Force

Take a few moments each day to drop into the feeling of your desired reality. Not just what it looks like, but how it feels. Do it until your body believes it. This trains your subconscious to recognize it as familiar and safe.

5. Aligned Action Over Forced Productivity

Every day, take one step—however small—that matches your future self. Not because you're trying to prove anything, but because this is who you are now.

6. End-of-Day Integration

Review your day through the lens of identity. Where did you act in alignment? Where did you revert to the old self? Reflect, not to shame—but to refine. This builds self-awareness and accelerates stabilization.

These practices are not add-ons. They are the structure that holds your frequency. Without them, you default to reaction. With them, you rise into embodiment.

You're Not Playing the Game—You Are the Game

When manifestation becomes a lifestyle, it's no longer a strategy you use when things aren't going your way. It's not a panic button. It's not a weekend workshop or a once-in-a-while vision board. It is how you live.

You begin to realize: every thought, every word, every boundary, every breath is part of the manifestation. Not because you're obsessively controlling your life—but because you've become conscious of your power.

You're no longer trying to manipulate reality. You're participating in it with presence and purpose. You're not chasing frequency—you are the frequency. And that frequency, sustained over time, shapes everything.

You walk differently. You speak differently. You choose differently. And your life, predictably, reflects those differences.

In the next and final Chapter, we'll close the loop on this journey—not with a technique, but with a truth. A truth that dissolves desire, not because it denies your dreams, but because it reveals what you were truly chasing all along: yourself.

And now, you're home.

Chapter 20: Your Final Unlock: Becoming the Manifestation

You've walked through every layer—emotion, identity, frequency, subconscious, energy, action. You've peeled back the illusions, released old timelines, and restructured your inner world to match the reality you want to live in. And now, at the end of this journey, comes the final shift. The final unlock.

You stop chasing the manifestation.

You become it.

The things you once longed for no longer live outside of you. You've embodied the frequency. You've stabilized the energy. You've cleared the static. You've remembered who you are. And in doing so, the desire dissolves—not because it didn't matter, but because you've merged with it so fully that there is no gap between you and the life you once envisioned.

This Chapter is not about more effort. It's about release. It's about stepping into the quiet certainty of a person who no longer needs to manifest anything—because they are the manifestation.

Desire Melts When Identity Matches It

At the beginning of your journey, your desires felt like faraway goals. They were outside of you—things to get, achieve, or attract. You wanted the money, the love, the clarity, the success. And so you began working toward them: learning the tools, practicing the alignment, doing the inner work.

But as your frequency rises, something powerful begins to happen. The desire doesn't disappear—it simply integrates. It no longer feels separate from you. You stop obsessing over when it's coming. You stop questioning if you're doing it right. You stop needing it to prove something.

That shift is not a loss of ambition. It's the gain of embodiment.

When your identity matches your desire, you no longer "want" it. You are it.

You're already living in the emotional and energetic state that the outcome represents. The house, the relationship, the career—it's already inside your field. And from there, the physical world catches up. Effortlessly. Naturally. Sometimes even anticlimactically.

Because the work has already been done.

Wanting is often a signal of separation. It says: "I'm here. That's there." But being? Being collapses the distance. Being turns vision into presence. And in presence, desire relaxes. Because there's nothing more to prove. There's nothing more to chase. There's only the unfolding of what has already been set in motion by your becoming.

Ask yourself: What would it look like if I stopped trying to get it and simply started being it?

Not acting "as if," but breathing, walking, and deciding as the version of you who no longer needs to want.

That's not fantasy. That's energetic mastery.

Your Life Reflects Your Self-Perception

By now, you understand that reality is not responding to what you say you want. It's responding to who you are being. And your being is shaped by your self-perception.

If you see yourself as unworthy, you will unconsciously repel what you say you desire. If you see yourself as the one who always struggles, you'll reinforce struggle, even when opportunities arise. If you see yourself as someone who almost gets there but never quite does, your life will mirror that exact frequency. But when you see yourself as powerful, capable, clear, and safe to receive—your world organizes itself around that inner image. Life becomes a reflection of self-concept. And that reflection is not static—it's alive, fluid, and always evolving.

Becoming the manifestation means upgrading your self-perception in a permanent way. You no longer visit alignment—you live in it. You no longer dip into confidence on good days—you carry it as your default. You no longer try to act like the version of you who has it—you simply are that version, without needing proof.

This doesn't mean perfection. It doesn't mean you never wobble. But even in the wobble, you know who you are. Even in uncertainty, you stay anchored. Because the manifestation is not something you're waiting for—it's something you're expressing.

When this truth lands, a new question emerges—not "How do I get it?" but "How do I become more of who I already am?"

That question opens the next Chapter of your evolution. It signals that you've stopped playing the manifestation game—and started creating from your essence.

The End of the Chase Is the Beginning of Real Power

The final unlock isn't flashy. It's not about a technique you haven't tried. It's not about optimizing your vision board or scripting your desires in a new way. It's about letting go of the chase entirely.

For so long, desire pulled you forward. It gave you direction, focus, and momentum. But now you've reached a frequency where the chase is no longer necessary. You are no longer hungry for outcomes. You are no longer negotiating your worth with the universe. You are no longer trading energy for validation. You've exited the loop.

This is where real power begins—not the power of control, but the power of presence. You walk into rooms differently. You speak from clarity. You don't overexplain, overwork, or overcompensate. You don't panic when plans change. You don't collapse when the outcome delays.

You hold.

You hold your vision, your frequency, your alignment—not because you need to, but because it's who you are now.

And this holding is what draws life toward you—not as a reward, but as a reflection.

When you stop chasing, your field becomes clear. Your nervous system becomes calm. Your magnetism becomes effortless. You are no longer vibrating at "almost"—you are vibrating at "already." And in that state, everything that once felt distant becomes obvious, available, and real.

Because it was never about chasing the thing.

It was always about becoming the version of you who doesn't have to.

You Are the Destination

If you've made it to this Chapter, you already know the truth.

The money was never the goal—it was the self-worth behind it.

The love was never the goal—it was the self-acceptance that allowed it.

The purpose was never the goal—it was the permission to be fully expressed.

The manifestation was never the goal—it was the becoming that made it possible.

And now you're here. Not because you mastered every step perfectly. But because you kept returning. To your center. To your clarity. To your power. Again and again, until the gap closed and the desire dissolved—not into disappointment, but into embodiment.

So what now?

You live. You create.

You expand—not because something is missing, but because wholeness wants to express itself through you.

You no longer chase. You no longer wait.

You walk—as the manifestation, not just of your vision, but of your truth

This is not the end.

It's the beginning.

And from here, everything is possible.

www.ingramcontent.com/pod-product-compliance
Lightning Source LLC
Chambersburg PA
CBHW070557160426
43199CB00014B/2532